Quality Living

Titles available in the Moody Elective Series:

The Basics of the Christian Life, by George Sweeting
Failure: The Back Door to Success, by Erwin W. Lutzer
The Freedom of Forgiveness, by David Augsburger
The God You Can Know, by Dan DeHaan
God's Answers to Man's Problems, by J. Dwight Pentecost
How in This World Can I Be Holy, by Erwin W. Lutzer
How to Interpret the Bible for Yourself, by Richard Mayhue
A Layman Looks at the Lord's Prayer, by W. Phillip Keller
Live Like a King, by Warren W. Wiersbe
Prayer Power Unlimited, J. Oswald Sanders
Quality Living, by Walter C. Kaiser
Understanding Bible Doctrine, by Charles C. Ryrie
Women and Their Emotions, by Miriam Neff
Your Family, by John MacArthur, Jr.
Your Power of Encouragement, by Jeanne Doering

Quality Living

by

Walter C. Kaiser, Jr.

MOODY PRESS
CHICAGO

© 1979 by
MOODY BIBLE INSTITUTE
OF CHICAGO

Original title: *Ecclesiastes: Total Life*

All rights reserved. No part of this book may be reproduced in any form without permission in writing from the publisher, except in the case of brief quotations embodied in critical articles or reviews.

All Scripture quotations, unless noted otherwise, are the author's translation.

Moody Press Elective Edition, 1986

Library of Congress Cataloging in Publication Data

Kaiser, Walter C.
  Quality living.

  (Moody elective series)
  Originally published: Ecclesiastes. Chicago: Moody Press, c1979.
  Bibliography: p.
  Includes index.
  1. Bible. O. T.   Ecclesiastes—Commentaries.
I. Title.
BS1475.3.K34   1986   223'.807   86-16398
ISBN 0-8024-7069-6 (pbk.)

1 2 3 4 5 6 7 Printing/DP/Year 91 90 89 88 87 86

Printed in the United States of America

Contents

CHAPTER   PAGE

   Preface   7
1. Introduction   11

Part 1: Enjoying Life as a Gift from God

2. The Restlessness of Life Illustrated   57
3. The Pleasures of Life Tested   61
4. The Purposes of Life Examined   69

Part 2: Understanding the All-Encompassing Plan of God

5. God's All Encompassing Plan   76
6. God's Plan Examined   84
7. Warnings Against Denying God's Plan   91

Part 3: Explaining and Applying God's Plan to the Lives of Believers

8. Evaluating Man's Outward Fortunes   100
9. Evaluating Man's Character   107
10. The Role of Human Government in God's Plan   112

Part 4: Removing Discouragements and Applying God's Plan to the Lives of Believers

11. Applying God's Plan to the Joy of Life   119
12. Applying God's Plan to Our Work   129
13. Death in View of God's Plan   147

   Selected Bibliography   159

To my former students at Wheaton College, Trinity Evangelical Divinity School, and Campus Crusade's Institute of Biblical Studies, for all the happy hours we spent together, working on the issue of Christ and culture.

Together we found the joy of discovery and the joy of life itself so clearly taught in Ecclesiastes.

To each of you I dedicate this set of studies, with special thanks to God for "the whole remembrance of you" (Philippians 1:3).

Preface

To the twentieth-century "man in the street," life is a puzzle. He feels that he, like his culture, has become plastic. For just as plastic now symbolizes the chief achievement of research, technocracy, and massive sales and distribution agencies, so also plastic people feel themselves to be the fruit of sociological research and constant manipulation by economic, political, social, and religious technocracies. Life has lost its zip. There is no joy in Mudville—or anywhere else. Man is made to feel cheap, commercial, dead, and machinelike. The basic worth and dignity of modern man are repeatedly denied when his humanity is deliberately overlooked and he is equated with the brutes and, worse still, with the machine. All the while, everything within that same man cries out for a larger view of the entirety of life.

Meanwhile his universe grows silent as he turns away from God, and twentieth-century man is gripped by an inexplicable loneliness. Is there no one home in the universe? Perhaps there is life on other planets. Surely if God is dead, as many depersonalized theologians say, echoing each other in their new, faceless roles, there must be someone or something else there. There has to be, or we are stuck.

But no, the agony, dread, nothingness, and boredom are worse than anyone had imagined. Truth with a capital *T* continues to disappear, almost in direct proportion to the disappearance of God from modern thought, "All is relative," goes the slogan, and that is the only absolute left.

The best illustration of what relativity means was forcefully brought to my attention as I attended a Danforth Teacher Study Grant Seminar fifteen years ago. During one of our seminars, an art teacher was asked to explain one of his oil paintings, as five other artists who preceded him had done. I will never forget his candor as he responded to a question about the message he intended to communicate in one of his expressionistic paintings with its swirls of dark browns, blacks, greens, and grays. He said, "When I finished painting this picture, I stepped back, and it didn't *say* anything to me. Then I turned it on its side, and still it didn't *say* anything to me." To my amazement, he concluded by saying, "So, I turned the picture upside down, and *that* is what I wanted to say!"

Only then did I fully begin to grasp what a terrific price was to be paid by modern men and women for the loss of truth and personal dignity. For the picture, created by a valuable, thinking, and creative artist who was made in the image of God, became the father of the painter. He, the creator, became shaped by his own creations! In his search for meaning, value, beauty, and the joy of the aesthetic, he was consumed by his own production.

Ecclesiastes is the best news around for such baffled modern men. It is the book for men who want to live again—*now*. It is the working man's book: it answers his boredom with the routine of joylessly eating, drinking, and earning a paycheck.

Ecclesiastes is also the thinking man's book. Its author knew that the thinking man is haunted by the questions, Who am I? What is the meaning of life? Should I be worldlier than thou or holier than thou? Or is there a third alternative that is simultaneously world accepting and God honoring?

Ecclesiastes has as its central concern that basic hunger of men to see if the totality of life fits into a meaningful pattern. Can this age of satanic rule and the eternal age to come both be accepted, enjoyed, and understood as parts of one plan? And if the same laws and plans of the omnipotent God apply to both ages, why does there often seem to be no divine plan in effect? Where are the goodness and joy of life in tragedy? Where is the sovereign direction of a wise, powerful, and good God when suffering Christians need Him most and seemingly He is not there?

Ecclesiastes was written to answer the above questions. It is in many ways a companion book to Job. And in other ways also it is a book of very unusual but desperately needed messages for this day. It is no wonder that of all the books of the Bible read by contemporary college students, this is the one that "turns them on" the most. There is good reason for that: it was written for people like them, and, in fact, for all of us.

My prayer is that the living God, who delights in restoring the joy of this life and the joy of eternal life to empty, plastic men and women of the twentieth century, will use Ecclesiastes and this new set of studies to provide a biblical definition of the relationship between Christ and culture. The need is as great for many believers who are held in cultural captivity as it is for unbelievers, who likewise swim in the eddies of our day and pursue pagan solutions to the questions of life and truth.

One final word before you open the text of Scripture and follow the comments in the pages that follow. In addition to sincerely acknowledging my gratitude to all my students during the past twenty years for the many happy hours spent in probing many of the questions dealt with in Ecclesiastes in all sorts of contexts and subjects, I must thank those who typed this manuscript with the same joy and wholehearted involvement as that taught in the book of Ecclesiastes. My thanks go to Mrs. Jenny Wiers, Mrs. Kathy Wiggins, and Mrs. Jan Olander. And with the pointed reminder in Ecclesiastes that my wife is a gift from God, I cheerfully acknowledge her encouragement and willingness to fill in the gaps while I was occupied with the hours of writing and research.

1

Introduction

THE UNITY OF THE BOOK

No book of the Bible has been so maligned and yet so misunderstood as the Old Testament book of Ecclesiastes. The most frequent assessment of the book is summed up in such negative terms as nihilistic, pessimistic, fatalistic, skeptical, cynical, materialistic, experimental, and the like.

But certainly those negative estimates reflect a superficial reading, for if the book is a unit, it also expresses an impressive list of positive ethical and spiritual injunctions. For instance, there are those repeated exhortations to (1) "fear God" (3:14; 5:7; 7:18; 8:12-13 [three times]; 12:13); (2) receive all the "good" things of life as a gift from God (2:24-26; 5:18-19; 8:15; 9:7-9); (3) reflect on the fact that God will judge the righteous and the wicked (3:17; 8:12-13; 11:9; 12:7*b*; 12:14); and (4) remember that God presently reviews the quality of every man's life-style (3:15*b*; 5:6*b*; 7:29; 8:5; 8:13; 11:9*b*; 12:1).

But pointing out a few positive exhortations in Ecclesiastes does not conclusively prove the unity of the book. Many interpreters suspect that the text of Ecclesiastes was worked and reworked precisely because, in their view, the positive ethical and spiritual sayings in the book are actually counter-balancing rationalizations for what they believe to be the overwhelmingly negative stance of the book as it was originally composed.

At least three fairly recent commentators (Carl Siegfried, *Goettinger Handkommentar,* 1898; A. H. McNeile, *An Introduction to Ecclesiastes,* 1904; and George A. Barton, *A Critical and Exegetical Commentary on the Book of Ecclesiastes,* 1908) agreed that corrective additions were made by two kinds of writers to the basic document originally written under the influence of what they considered to be Greek philosophical thought: a "wisdom writer" *ḥakam* and a "pious interpolator" *ḥasid.* In the former category, the three commentators agreed that the following texts should be regarded as additions made by the "wisdom writer": 4:5; 7:11, 12, 19; 8:1; 9:17-18; 10:3, 12-14*a,* 15. There were many other texts suggested as the work of "the wisdom writer," but on the above list the commentators all concurred. Those texts are isolated proverbs, dealing with life and nature, that corrected and enlarged the original document of Ecclesiastes—so it was argued.

There are also those passages attributed to a "pious redactor" (or "pious interpolator"). From the passages suggested, the three scholars agreed on the following list of suspected additions from his pen: 2:26*a*; 3:17; 7:29; 8:2*b*-3*a*, 5-6*a*, 11-13; 11:9*b*; 12:1*a.* Most interpreters who believe Ecclesiastes was reworked add the epilogue of 12:13-14 to this same class, although other commentators attribute it to a fourth writer. Those who believe in the fourth writer think that some religiously inclined Jewish reader of Ecclesiastes "graciously" added some teaching on divine judgment, the divine source of all that exists, and the divine source of all that happens as a mild improvement on an otherwise dreary text.

Whether Ecclesiastes is the work of more than one writer is, of course, exactly the point that needs to be debated. What is the evidence for multiple authorship of the text? None of our present Hebrew textual traditions suggests any division of labor; instead the unity of the document is everywhere attested by all Hebrew manuscripts.

How then shall the matter be settled? Must the result be left to each reader's own preference; some finding that Ecclesiastes teaches only pessimism, gloom, and doubt, whereas others extract a message of cheerful industry and enjoyment of life as a gift from God?

A proper perspective on any book demands that we first come to terms with the author's intention. We must be able to state the author's purpose, plan, and scope. There are three places to which we can go to obtain that information. We can read the preface or introduction to a book; we can flip quickly to the concluding chapter, especially if it is a mystery and we wish to know "who done it"; or we can skim the contents of the work for any repeated refrains or special hobbyhorses.

THE AUTHOR'S EPILOGUE

Setting aside the prologue of Ecclesiastes for the moment, the epilogue in 12:8-14 is the most significant clue about what the book is attempting to do. The inattentive and superficial reader might mistake what some regard as the collection of loose and detailed sentences in Ecclesiastes as a sign that the book is without any coherence or orderly design. But once the epilogue is accepted as an original part of the book, that argument evaporates.

Because most commentators doubt that there is any direct relationship between the epilogue and the body of Ecclesiastes, it must be demonstrated that there is an intimate connection between the vocabulary and basic ideology of the two parts. Among the more prominent links is the theme of 12:14, namely, that there is an appointed time when God will execute His justice, a theme that also exists in 11:9.

> 12:14: "God will bring every deed into judgment."
>
> 11:9: "Know that for all these things God will bring you into judgment."

The same promise is given elsewhere in the book.

> 3:17: "God will judge the righteous and the wicked, for He appointed a time for every matter and for every work."
>
> 9:1: "The righteous and the wise and their deeds are in the hand of God" (cf. 5:8; 12:7).

Likewise, the command "to fear God" (Elohim) found in 12:13 is intimately linked with the same command in 3:14; 5:7; 7:18; and 8:12-13 (three times). We must conclude then that these two great themes, fearing God and an appointed time for divine judgment, were not innovative features introduced in the last two verses of the book. Resisting this evidence leads to consistently stripping the rest of the book of all spiritual and ethical affirmations. Such radical literary surgery exposes itself to the charge of being subjective and somewhat prejudicial in its canon of literary criticism, for it cares for its problems by ruling them out of order on internal and definitional grounds.

If, as I have argued, a fair case can be made for the unity and integral connection of the epilogue to the rest of the book, then Ecclesiastes does have a deliberate and consciously pursued conclusion: "The sum [*sop*] of the matter" (12:13*a*). There is a conclusion to the "whole thing" (*hakkol*), and the author proceeds to give the theme and purpose of his whole book.

Surprisingly enough, it is not "All is vanity"; instead, it is to "fear God and keep His commandments," for the entirety (*kol*) of personality (the "manishness" of man and "womanness" of woman) is found in this single injunction.

Furthermore, the epilogue asserts that the substance of Ecclesiastes came from the pen of one who was "wise" (12:9). What he wrote was nothing less than "words of truth" (12:10), "written in uprightness" (12:10) and couched in "pleasant words," or "words of delight" (12:10). Surely the author's estimate of his own labors, in which "he taught the people knowledge, weighed and studied proverbs with great care" (12:9), hardly gives credence to those who accuse him of being guilty of reasoning after the manner of a natural man immersed in pessimism, skepticism, materialism, fatalism, and the like.

Nor was the work of the author of Ecclesiastes the result of mere experience and experimentalism, for the "saying of the wise," in which category he placed his own work in 12:9, were "given by one Shepherd" (12:11). It hardly seems possible to equate this reference to "one Shepherd" to anyone other than Jehovah, that is, Yahweh, the Shepherd of Israel. That title of our Lord is found in almost every period of Israel's long history in Scripture (Genesis 48:15; 49:24; Psalm 23:1; Isaiah 40:11; Jeremiah 31:10; Ezekiel 34:11-12).[1] Therefore, Ecclesiastes has its source in divine revelation just as surely as does any other book of the Bible that claims to be the result of "thus saith the Lord." The claim to divine inspiration could not be plainer or more boldly stated. Ecclesiastes came from the Lord and not human experience.

THE AUTHOR'S THEME

Even among those who admit that Ecclesiastes has a single theme, there are wide differences of opinion over what that theme is, because so many commentators put an undue emphasis on one or another part of the book or class of passages in it. Jerome used the book to teach the young woman from Rome named Blessila the vanity of this present world and that she should choose instead a life of monasticism—all this in spite of Qoheleth's advice to eat, drink, and enjoy life as a gift from God. Conversely, others have focused solely on this last piece of advice and concluded

---

1. Herbert C. Leupold, *Exposition of Ecclesiastes* (Columbus, Ohio: Wartburg, 1952), p. 295.

that worldly pleasure is the highest good. Now Ecclesiastes cannot teach that both monasticism and worldly pleasure are the chief good, unless the author were hopelessly involved in a string of self-contradictions and conundrums.

Offering a third view of the theme of Ecclesiastes, others have incorrectly drawn theories of fatalism from attaching an undue prominence and incorrect understanding to such passages as 1:4-11; 3:1-15; 7:13-14; and 9:11, where the fixed order of things in the universe is linked with the plan and will of God. But Qoheleth never denied the freedom of man and thereby argued for confusion and disorder; nor did he suggest that there was an unalterable plan of God over all things that was to be the overriding theme of his book.

Qoheleth was working on the problem of man's attempt to find meaning in all aspects of God's good world without coming to know the world's Creator, Sustainer and final Judge. For central to all of man's concerns is this problem of integrating life and truth.

The issue appears to have come to a head in 3:11:

> [God] has made everything beautiful in its time; he has also put eternity [*òlam*] into man's heart so that he cannot find out what God has done from beginning to the end.

And there are issue hangs. Man has a capacity and desire to know how all things, men, and ideas fit together—the end from the beginning—and yet he cannot know until he comes to know the One who built man in His own image with the capacity to understand who he is as a man, what he means, and what is the worth of things, even life itself. Life, in and of itself, even God's good world with all its good, God-given gifts, is unable to deliver meaning and joy when it is appropriated in a piecemeal fashion. This, as will be argued later on, is the meaning of the prologue: "Vanity of vanities, all is vanity"; namely, that no single part of God's good world can unlock the meaning to life. Life, in and of itself, is unable to supply the key to the questions of identity, meaning, purpose, value, enjoyment, and destiny. Only in coming to know God can one begin to find answers to these questions.

Especially difficult in trying to understand the meaning of life is the problem of the apparent inequities of divine providence. How can the justice of God be reconciled with the seemingly unmitigated prosperity of the wicked (7:14-15)? Nevertheless, man's entire welfare even in this area continues to depend on one thing: whether that person fears God and keeps His commandments, for God will bring every work into judgment—both good and evil. Therefore, all present appearances to the contrary will not be properly understood if this kind of reckoning is excluded.

THE AUTHOR'S REFRAINS

That this analysis is the one set forth by the author of Ecclesiastes can also be determined from a set of refrains that recurs throughout the entire argument. Six times this refrain appears: "Eat and drink and make your soul enjoy good of its labor, for it is a gift of God" (2:24; 3:12-13; 3:22; 5:18-19; 8:15; 9:7-9). That this is no Epicurean sentiment has already been argued.

However, some would discourage us from the objective of laying out the scope and plan of the book by contending that the writer had no such goal in mind. Even the conservative Franz Delitzsch agreed with this negative judgment:

> A gradual development, a progressive demonstration, is wanting, and even the grouping together of the parts is not fully carried out; the connection of thoughts . . . is external and accidental. . . . All attempts to show, in the whole, not only oneness of spirit, but a generic progress, an all embracing plan, and an organic connection have hitherto failed, and must fail.[2]

Likewise, the conservative E. W. Hengstenberg said:

> A connected and orderly argument, an elaborate arrangement of parts, is as little to be looked for here as in the special portion of the Book of Proverbs which begins with Chapter X; or as in the alphabetical Psalms.[3]

It is, of course, conceivable that the writer discussed his theme without any orderly arrangement or methodological outline of its various parts. He *may have*

---

2. Franz Delitzsch, *Commentary on the Song of Songs and Ecclesiastes,* trans. M. G. Easton (1877; reprinted in *Biblical Commentary on the Old Testament,* by C. F. Keil and Franz Delitzsch, Grand Rapids: Eerdmans, 1950), p. 188.
3. Ernst W. Hengstenberg, *Commentary on Ecclesiastes,* trans. D. W. Simon (Philadelphia: Smith, English, 1860), p. 15.

just jotted down thoughts as they came to him rather spontaneously or as one idea provoked an associated concept, all without any logical sequence. On the other hand, he did come to a "summary" and a "conclusion," or an "end," to his whole work in 12:13-14. Furthermore, he signaled the links in the progress of his thought through various repeated refrains. Thus we must conclude that it is unlikely that he had no plan or outline in mind as he set forth his work. His own words indicate otherwise.

THE AUTHOR'S LOGIC AND THE PRESERVATION OF HIS TEXT

Some commentators will grant that the author had a general plan in mind as he wrote, but they say that he also indulged in a number of digressions that are really incidental to his main argument. It was either that, those writers contend, or the original plan was frustrated by a poor transcription and a general disarrangement of the original sequence of the text through the work of some copyist of the biblical text.

Again, however, the suppositions are groundless. There is no reason to allege such textual corruption or transpositions of sections in the present text. As for the alleged digressions, which apparently would play no part in the central theme of the book, the claim of their existence may be answered best by showing that there is clear plan to the whole book as it stands. In an unsigned article in *The Princeton Review*, a writer convincingly argued:

> There is a clear and consistent plan in the book of Ecclesiastes, which needs no changes nor mutilations

... to [expedite] its discovery; one, in fact, of the most strictly logical and methodical kind. Not only is the argument well conducted, conclusive and complete but its various points are so admirably disposed, its divisions so regular, and its different parts so conformed in structure, as to give evidence that the whole was carefully considered and well digested before it was put together. This differs perhaps from the prevalent opinion, but we are convinced that they who complain of a want of method, *haerent in cortice*.[4]

THE AUTHOR'S OUTLINE

There have been an almost infinite number of schemes suggested for discerning the outline of Ecclesiastes. Without citing all the scholarly apparatus, we can summarize the key divisions among the scholars to be between those who argue for *two* sections (of equal parts: six chapters each; or unequal parts: four chapters and eight) and those who find *three* sections (of four chapters each—or even *four* divisions (chaps. 1-2; 3-5; 6-8:15; 8:16—12:14).

The twofold division is usually based on the principle that the first part of Ecclesiastes contains the theoretical portion and the second the practical aspects of the subject. Therefore, the vanity of all earthly things is established in part one, and then part two points out what duties and obligations such truth should elicit from mankind.

It is true that the book becomes more practical and filled with exhortation toward the end, but the separa-

---

4. "The Scope and Plan of the Book of Ecclesiastes," *The Princeton Review* (1857): 427. The Latin phrase means "are stuck in the mud."

tion between doctrine and practice is not that sharp in the book. Practical applications are being made already in 2:24-26; 3:10-15, 17, 22; and 5:1-7, 18-20.

The most satisfactory division of Ecclesiastes is one that separates the text into four parts. Hitzig's suggestion that there are three parts is an attempt to mediate between the twofold and fourfold divisions (*The Preacher Solomon Explained*, 1847). But his suggestion must be rejected because it awkwardly breaks the text, clumsily drawing divisions that override the stylistic hints and the unity of arguments set forth by the writer of Ecclesiastes.

I was deeply impressed with the breakdown of Ecclesiastes in the previously mentioned article in the *Princeton Review*, which in turn follows Vaihinger's *Studien und Kritiken* (1848), which Keil had also used in his *Introduction* (1849). This division of Ecclesiastes is as follows:

> Part I   1:2—2:26
> Part II 3:1—5:20
> Part III 6:1—8:15
> Part IV 8:16—12:14

The most obvious advantage the above fourfold division has is that each of the first three sections climaxes with a formal refrain that is given in almost identical terms: "To eat and drink and to realize the benefit of one's labor" is all a gift from God (2:24; 5:18; 8:15).

In 1849, J. G. Vaihinger had argued:

> The design of the Preacher is to propound the immorality of the soul, wherein alone the solution of the otherwise inexplicable problems of life are happily to be found; and to encourage us to look forward to a future judgment, amid the discrepancies between the moral nature and fate of man.[5]

The way Vaihinger analyzed the development of this theme was to view the book as

> four interwoven poetico-dialectic discourses, all treating upon the same theme, viz, the vanity of human life, as well as the object and aim of it. Each discourse consists of three parts, which are again subdivided into strophes and half strophes. . . .
>
> DISCOURSE I. (chap. i.2-ii.26) shews that by the eternal, unalterably fixed course of all earthly things, and the experience of the vain and unsatisfactory strivings after earthly wisdom and selfish gratifications, a god-fearing enjoyment of life, and accepting gratefully the present good, can alone constitute the end of our earthly existence.
>
> DISCOURSE II. (chap. iii. 1-v. 19) shews that by the experience that all our effort in the world depend upon time and circumstances, and that the success of human labour is altogether controlled by circumstances, the cheerful enjoyment of life, connected with the fear of

---

5. J. G. Vaihinger in Christian D. Ginsburg, *Coheleth, Commonly Called the Book of Ecclesiastes* (1861; reprinted in *The Song of Songs and Coheleth (Commonly Called the Book of Ecclesiastes,* The Library of Biblical Studies, ed. Harry M. Orlinsky, New York: Ktav, 1970), p. 221.

> God and humility, is to be recommended as the highest good.
>
> DISCOURSE III. (chap. vi. 1-viii.15) shews that by the observation that man is frequently deprived of the enjoyment of riches, acquired through the favour of God, either from the fault of others or his own, we must try a nobler way to procure the real and cheerful enjoyment of life, by joyfully using earthly blessings following higher wisdom, and avoiding folly.
>
> DISCOURSE IV. (chap. viii. 16-xii.8), considering the melancholy experience of the inscrutable government of God in the distribution of human destinies, nothing remains to us, besides the exercise of wisdom and the fear of God, for the quieting of our minds, but in looking forward to a retributive eternity, and to an otherwise cheerless old age, cheerfully and gratefully to enjoy the good and the beautiful in life, especially in our youth and in the vigour of our manhood.[6]

Vaihinger handicapped what in many ways was an excellent treatise with his predilection for finding strophes of equal length. That penchant caused him to lose the real argument of the book and develop an artificial thought pattern at several critical points. His overriding concern for mechanical regularity of strophes cost him a proper understanding of the internal divisions of the thought, even though he divided the sections properly.

The unsigned article in the 1857 *Princeton Review* immeasurably improved on Vaihinger's arrangement

---

6. Ibid., pp. 221-22.

Introduction 25

of the argument of Ecclesiastes. There was agreement with Vaihinger on the fourfold division of the book. But the argument proceeded in this fashion:

I. (Chapter i.2-ii.26) A Preliminary argument from Solomon's own experience designed to show that happiness is not in man's own power; that all striving and toiling, though it may surround him with every gratification his heart can desire, is powerless to give that gratification itself.

II. (Chapter iii.1-v.20). [God] has a scheme in which every event and all the multifarious actions of men, with the time of their occurrence are definitely arranged. This scheme is, 3:11, a beautiful one, though from their prevailing worldliness men do not comprehend it. . . . He next proceeds to allege various facts . . . [or] anomali [es which] . . . seem to be so serious an exception to his grand doctrine that justice rules in the world and happiness attends right-doing . . . [that] He first utters a caution against being seduced to irreligion, to neglect of religious duty, or to inconsiderate language reflecting upon God's providence by such contemplations. . . . These wrongs, which are acknowledged to exist, find redress, therefore, in superior government human and divine.

III. (Chapter vi.1-viii.15) The next step, and this constitutes the central portion of the whole book, is to apply this [i.e., that enjoyment of the world is a gift of God, bestowed by God and regulated by His grand plan] to the explanation of the inequalities of divine providence. . . . Prosperity may not be a good. . . . And adversity or affliction is not necessarily an evil.... A right application of the considerations ... will remove a large proportion of the apparent inequalities of providence.

IV. Chapters viii.16-xii.14) The fourth section ... is occupied with the removal of discouragements and the enforcing of practical lessons.... The remaining mystery of this subject need be no obstacle to human joy... nor to strenuous activity ... while in both their joy and their activity men should be mindful of death and judgment.... The conclusion of the entire discussion is stated to be: Fear God and keep His commandments; for this is the whole welfare of man; for God shall bring every work into judgment; with every secret thing, whether it be good or whether it be evil.[7]

THE WRITER, THE ADDRESSES, THE TIMES, AND THE CANONICAL STATUS OF HIS WORK

Some attention should be given to the title, author, audience, and circumstances under which Ecclesiastes was written. Also, the matter of canonicity should be discussed.

THE NAME QOHELETH

Seven times the writer gives to himself the name Qoheleth: three times at the beginning (1:1, 2, 12), three times at the end (12:8, 9, 10), and once in the

---

7. "The Scope and Plan of the Book of Ecclesiastes," pp. 428, 431-32, 433-36, 437-38, 440.

middle (7:27). Because Qoheleth appears with the article in 12:8, and especially because it takes a feminine verb in 7:27, it cannot be a proper name of some individual, but instead must be an appellative, that is, a designation of some sort. In form, it is an active feminine participle from the Hebrew verb *qahal*, meaning "to call," then "to call together, to assemble, to collect."

For some, the feminine form of Qoheleth indicated that the word was an abstract designation of an office, the designation being transferred to the person holding that official privilege. But although it is true that feminine forms sometimes express abstracts, Ginsburg complains that they are never formed from the active participle.[8] Keil would have responded with the difficult examples of Nehemiah 7:57 (*Sophereth* meaning "scribe") and Ezra 2:57 (*Pokereth* meaning "gazelle-tender"), which are actually proper names in those two contexts.[9]

Therefore, it seems best to understand "Qoheleth" as describing the act of gathering the people together. That definition matches the use of *qahal* in numerous other biblical passages, where it is invariably used for assembling *people,* especially for spiritual purposes. Therefore, other interpretations (such as sophist, philosopher, preacher, compiler or collector, penitent, old man, exclaiming voice, departed spirit, eclectic, and academy) are to be rejected.

8. Ginsburg, p. 9.
9. Karl F. Keil, *Manual of Historico-Critical Introduction to the Canonical Scriptures of the Old Testament,* trans. George C. M. Douglas, 2 vols. (Edinburgh: T. & T. Clark, 1869-70), 1:513.

IDENTITY OF THE WRITER

Who then was the author who gathered the people together to hear this book? In 1:12 the writer said, "I, Qoheleth, became king over Israel in Jerusalem," and in 1:1 the book was prefaced with the claim, "The words of Qoheleth, son of David, king in Jerusalem." Because Solomon was the only immediate son of David who was king over Israel, reigning in Jerusalem, there can be little doubt that he is the one so specified. Yet the conservative Franz Delitzsch said, "If the Book of *Koheleth* were of old Solomonic origin, then there is no history of the Hebrew language."[10] And a contemporary scholar Robert Gordis, is just as definite about the whole matter:

> The view that Solomon is the author has been universally abandoned today, with the growth of a truer recognition of the style, vocabulary and world-outlook of Koheleth.[11]

Nevertheless, even C. D. Ginsburg recognized that Solomonic authorship is "fully corroborated by the unequivocal allusions made throughout this book to particular circumstances connected with the life of this great monarch."[12] Ginsburg invited us to compare, for instance:

Ecclesiastes 1:16 with 1 Kings 3:12 (showing Solomon's unrivaled wisdom);

---

10. Delitzsch, p. 190.
11. Robert Gordis, *Koheleth* (New York: Schocken, 1968), p. 5.
12. Ginsburg, p. 244.

Ecclesiastes 2:4-10 with 1 Kings 5:27-32;
Ecclesiastes 2:4-10 with 1 Kings 7:1-8 (showing Solomon's unsurpassed wealth);
Ecclesiastes 2:4-10 with 1 Kings 9:17-19 (showing Solomon's huge retinue of servants);
Ecclesiastes 2:4-10 with 1 Kings 10:14-29 (showing Solomon's extensive building operations);
Ecclesiastes 7:20 with 1 Kings 8:46 ("There is no man who does not sin.");
Ecclesiastes 7:28 with 1 Kings 11:1-8 (not a God-fearing woman among a thousand); and
Ecclesiastes 12:9 with 1 Kings 4:32 (showing Solomon to be weighing, studying, and arranging proverbs).[13]

Still the issue is pressed: perhaps Solomon is the personated author, that is, the actor in whose mouth a later writer placed sentiments that suited him, rather than the real author of the book. The absence of explicit claims of Solomonic authorship found in other works (e.g., the Proverbs of Solomon; the Song of Songs, which is Solomon's; or the Psalms of Solomon—Psalms 72 and 127) is thought to be extremely significant, especially since the title is probably introduced to indicate an ideal or representative role. Qoheleth is consistently used instead of a proper name.

But 1:12 becomes the most important piece of evidence to be used in arguing against the Solomonic authorship of this book. The sacred writer represents Solomon as saying that in the *past*, "I *was* king over Israel in Jerusalem." The writer used the perfect tense of the verb "to be" (*hayiti*). Thus it is said that Solo-

---

13. Ibid.

mon was no longer king when this text was composed.

The above argument will not bear all the weight it is called to bear. The perfect tense actually denotes a state of action that began in the past and stretches forward to the present. Only in later Hebrew is it restricted to past events. This form of the verb would be proper even if Solomon were writing. For as George Barton noted, it was used by Moses when he named his son Gershom ("sojourner"—I *"was,"* or better still *"have been,"* a sojourner in a foreign land [Exodus 2:22] and by pleading brothers to an unrecognized Joseph: "We are all sons of one man, we are honest men, your servants *were* not [or have not been] spies" (Genesis 42:11.[14] So Solomon could have said "I have been king." Thus we see that Hebrew can be deliberately indefinite about the time aspect of a verb, and that was the way the author wanted it in 1:12.

But 1:12 is not the only passage presenting an alleged difficulty to Solomonic authorship. In 1:16 the writer compares himself advantageously "over all who were before me in Jerusalem." Since David was the only Hebrew ruler to precede Solomon in Jerusalem, the words are hardly appropriate in Solomon's mouth—so the argument goes. But Hengstenberg[15] argued that even if the phrase is limited to kings, the reference is probably to the line of Canaanite kings who preceded Solomon in Jerusalem, such as Mel-

---

14. George A. Barton, *A Critical and Exegetical Commentary on the Book of Ecclesiastes* (1908; reprinted in The International Critical Commentary, ed. Samuel R. Driver, Alfred Plummer, and Charles A. Briggs, Edinburgh: T. & T. Clark, 1959), p. 85.
15. Hengstenberg, pp. 60-61.

chizedek (Genesis 14:18), Adonizedec (Joshua 10:1), and Araunah (2 Samuel 24:23). That easily cares for the issue.

A single argument left in favor of a post-Solomonic origin for Ecclesiastes is the character of its language. On this basis, even such conservative scholars as Hengstenberg, Delitzsch, Leupold, and E. J. Young felt compelled to date the book in the fifth century B.C., and others placed it in the Greek period from the third century B.C. to the time of Herod the Great.

Here again, however, the linguistic evidence does not support the conclusion reached. The complete absence of any Hebrew vowels points to an exceptionally early composition of the book. Final vowel letters (*matres lectionis*) first appeared in the late eighth century B.C. and medial, or middle, vowel letters came into vogue at the end of the seventh or early sixth century B.C.[16]

Furthermore, many of the twenty-nine alleged Aramaisms are actually of Canaanite-Phoenician vintage, according to Mitchell Dahood.[17] In fact, it is almost impossible to avoid the conviction that Ecclesiastes is of such a unique and special genre that it currently fits into no known period of the history of the Hebrew language. Archer and Dahood both repeat Jastrow's and Margoliouth's judgment that it is impossible to explain the peculiarities of Qoheleth's grammar, syntax, and orthography on the basis that it is late Mish-

16. Gleason Archer, "The Linguistic Evidence for the Date of 'Ecclesiastes,'" *Journal of the Evangelical Theological Society* 12 (1969): 171.
17. Mitchell Dahood, "Canaanite-Phoenician Influence in Qoheleth," *Biblica* 33 (1952): 201-2.

naic Hebrew or late Aramaic.[18] To support his judgment, Margoliouth pointed to (1) the frequency of the participial present; (2) the ungarbled, but nonetheless unintelligible nature of certain phrases in later times; (3) the complete omission of the name Yahweh; (4) the failure to allude to anything from previous Hebrew history; and (5) the absence of any of the newer Jewish words for "business," "lest," or "authorize."

But if the internal evidence, with its similarities to the phrases, style of life, and experience of the Davidic King Solomon depicted in 1 Kings 1-11, and the external linguistic evidence argue for orthography, lexicography, and even syntax that may reach back into the tenth century B.C., there is no reason why we should not conclude that the writer and speaker was Solomon, son of King David.

The predominant ideas found in Ecclesiastes, namely, wisdom and the fear of God, and their application to secular and sacred life likewise fit the character of Solomon as set forth in 1 Kings 3 and the book of Proverbs.

THE DATE AND PURPOSE OF ECCLESIASTES

At what stage in Solomon's life did he write Ecclesiastes? And what was his purpose in writing the book? The book would appear to best fit that period of Solomon's life when his love for his Lord was stolen by his practice of idolatry and his outrageous viola-

---

18. Archer, p. 170: Dahood, pp. 30-31; Morris Jastrow, Jr. and David S. Margoliouth, "The Book of Ecclesiastes," in *The Jewish Encyclopedia*, ed. Isidore Singer, 12 vols. (New York: Funk and Wagnalls, 1901-6), 5:33.

tion of the principle of monogamous marriage. So, in part, went the Jewish legend with its Aramaic paraphrase of 1:12:

> When King Solomon was sitting upon the throne of his kingdom, his heart became greatly elated with riches, and he transgressed the commandment of the Word of God; and he gathered many houses, and chariots, and riders, and he amassed much gold and silver, and he married wives from foreign nations. Whereupon the anger of the Lord was kindled against him, and he sent to him Ashmodai, the king of the demons, and he drove him from the throne of his kingdom, and took away the ring from his hand, in order that he should roam and wander about in the world, to reprove it; and he went about the provincial towns and cities in the land of Israel, weeping and lamenting, and saying, "I am Coheleth, whose name was formerly called Solomon, who was King over Israel in Jerusalem."[19]

The introduction of Ashmodai, king of the demons, and a period of dethronement are, of course, subbiblical and call for no further comment. But the connection of Solomon's sinful backsliding with the occasion of the book is at least noteworthy. Could it be that the picture of old age in 12:1-6 contains the autobiographical mark?

Solomon was given another name from the Lord when he was born—Jedidiah, "Beloved of the Lord" (2 Samuel 12:24-25). Indeed, he was promised per-

---

19. Targum on Ecclesiastes 1:12 and The Jerusalem Talmud, tractate Sanhedrin 20 c.

sonal adoption and mercy as God's own son (2 Samuel 7:14-15). Yet the Lord was angry with His "son" when "his heart had turned away from the Lord, the God of Israel" (1 Kings 11:9). Therefore, the Lord "appeared to him twice" (1 Kings 11:9). Then he "raised up adversar[ies] against him" (1 Kings 11:14, 23, 26) and used them as the rod of affliction to turn Solomon from his backsliding.

Did those measures have any effect? And is the book of Ecclesiastes a witness to any possible effect that all those divine evidences of the love of God had on his life? The answer to both questions is yes. There is in the book an air of repentance and humility for past values and performance. Then there is the matter of later books using both David and Solomon as models for the expected Messianic kingdom (1 and 2 Chronicles or as the "way"; that is, the life-styles of both David and Solomon were considered to be worthy of emulation (2 Chronicles 11:17). The reference to Solomon's "wisdom" even in the "rest of his days" could be a reference to the end of his life (1 Kings 11:41).

The writer of 1 Kings 11:41 assured his readers that the record of the rest of what Solomon "did and his wisdom" was written in "the book of acts of Solomon." Although some have wondered out loud if Ecclesiastes might be the book referred to in 1 Kings 11:41, that would appear to be improbable, because no such title as "The Acts of Solomon" has ever been found to be attached to any known manuscript of Ecclesiastes. Nevertheless, that Solomon did experience repentance and restoration, even as did that Davidite Manasseh (which was a reversal of a half century of evil and sin), would have gone unnoticed had not a relatively small, later footnote been included in 2 Chronicles 33:18-20. Therefore, given the Solomonic authorship of the book, it will be best placed *not before* his apostasy, for the questions and sins of Ecclesiastes did not trouble him then, not *during* his years of rebellion, for then he had no occasion to use the language of spiritual things. Ecclesiastes is best placed *after* his apostasy, when both his recent turmoil and repentance were still fresh in his mind.

Why, then, it may be asked, was Solomon so stingy with his references to Yahweh's previous mercies to Israel? Indeed, the book may be further faulted in that (1) it never used the covenant name of Yahweh, but rather twenty-eight times used Elohim (God), a name generally used when there is reference to God's work as Creator and Sustainer for all men apart from any work of grace in salvation; (2) there is no mention of the Mosaic law; and (3) there is no treatment of any aspect of the special features of God's call or guidance of Israel in her history.

One idea that goes a long way toward answering the "faults" in the paragraph above is that Solomon may have intentionally written Ecclesiastes with an eye to a wider circle of readers than just the Hebrews—perhaps those Aramaean and other Semitic nations that were then subject to his government and those nations that had caused a good deal of his spiritual downfall through his attempt to placate the numerous wives who hailed from them. Such a "cosmopolitan tendency" would be most appropriate for Wisdom Literature of the Bible, which had the aim of raising a voice to "the sons of men" at large so that all might hear (Proverbs 8:4). The book would then have a missionary flavor as it attempted to use a sort of what we now call "cultural apologetics" to call Gentiles at large to straighten out their thinking, acting, values, and preparation for their eternal destiny. The point of contact with those pagans would be the ancient hope, "O that we might see some good!" (Psalm 4:6), or the questions of Micah 6:6 and Deuteronomy 10:12: "With what shall I come before the Lord?" and, "What does the Lord your God require of you?"

Had not the Queen of Sheba heard of the famed wisdom of Solomon and his ability to answer difficult questions (1 Kings 10:1)? It may be surmised that requests such as hers provided the reason for making a discussion like Ecclesiastes available to a wider audience. Thus the fundamental principles, or first steps, in godliness were set forth for those who had the longest spiritual road to travel. A "missionary message" to the Gentiles would have to begin with those issues that affect all men because all share the image of God and yet are involved in a world that is often unintelligible and hostile.

The call for such a treatise as this was also to be found in the directive given by Moses in Deuteronomy 4:6-8:

> Keep [my statutes and commandments] and do them; for that will be your wisdom and your discernment *in the eyes of the peoples,* who *when they hear all these statutes, will say,* "What a wise and discerning people is this great nation!" Where is there a great nation that has a god so near to it as the Lord our God is whenever we call on him? Where is there a great nation that

has statutes and ordinances so fair as this whole law which I am placing before you today? (emphasis added).

Solomon was eminently qualified to set forth wisdom before the "eyes of the peoples" at large, just as he had done in Proverbs. Instead of being transformed by the culture of his subject nations and Gentile allies, he would begin with the very basic questions of life: What is good? What is worthwhile? What is life meant to accomplish? How can anyone satisfy that gnawing thirst to find out the end from the beginning and bridge that "eternity" in the heart of all men (3:11)?

On the other hand, the book must not be viewed as being totally out of keeping with the distinctive message found in the progress of divine revelation up to that time of the united monarchy at approximately 1000 B.C. One of the central points of the book is one of the keys that connects Ecclesiastes to the theology of previous texts: Fear God, for this is what life is all about. The book of Deuteronomy had made "the fear of the Lord" a focal point of concern (Deuteronomy 4:10; 5:29; 6:2, 13, 24; 8:6; 10:12, 20; 13:4; 14:23; 17:19; 28:58; 31:12-13). Indeed, "To fear the Lord" was to commit oneself to Yahweh by faith, as did *some* of the Egyptians (Exodus 9:20, 30) who formed part of the mixed multitude that left Egypt with Israel (Exodus 12:38). That fear was not some extraordinary, numinous feeling of terror or even of awe, but instead it was an attitude of receptivity that manifested itself in belief, obedience, and love for the living God. That attitude had already appeared—on Mount

Moriah when Abraham willingly offered his son Isaac (Genesis 22:12) and in Joseph's believing response (Genesis 42:18). If Job is to be placed in the patriarchal era, then he, too, must be cited as an early example of what our book of Ecclesiastes is urging (Job 1:1, 8-9; 2:3). Another example is the midwives who evidenced the same attitude of obedient faith (Exodus 1:17, 21). In fact, to fear God is to live—and to live more abundantly (Leviticus 19:14, 32; 25:17, 36, 43; Proverbs 10:27; 14:27; 19:23; 22:4). Such teaching about the "fear of the Lord" is "a fountain of life" (Proverbs 13:14; 14:27). Why should man, created by God in His image, joylessly endure life as a burden, only to finally face the judgment of God as a further blow after having missed purpose, joy, and the meaning of this life?

The second mark of continuity in Ecclesiastes with previous Scripture is the injunction to "keep His commandments." Failure to do so will not only rob the rebel of his present enjoyment of that list of earthly blessings promised in Leviticus 26 and Deuteronomy 28 to all who would walk in the way of the Lord; but disobedience to God's commandments will also expose the wicked "every day," as well as in that final day, to the anger and judgments of God (Psalm 7:11). The prominence of judgment in the book of Ecclesiastes is seen easily from the following citations:

3:17: The righteous and the wicked God will judge.
5:6b: Why should God be angry at your voice and destroy the work of your hands?
8:12-13: Although a sinner does evil a hundred times and protracts his life, yet I know it will be well with

those fearing God because they fear in His presence. But it will not be well with the wicked, neither will be protract his days like a shadow, because there is no fear in the presence of God.

11:9b: But know that for all these things [walking in the ways of your heart] God will bring you into judgment.

12:7b: The spirit returns to God who gave it.

12:4: For God shall bring every work to judgment with every secret deed, whether good or evil.

The most startling text is 11:9, which some say directly contradicts Numbers 15:39b: 'You shall remember all the commandments of the Lord and obey them and not follow after your own heart and your own eyes, which you are inclined to go after lustily." The men who produced Codex B of the Greek translation of the Old Testament (the Septuagint) reacted so strongly to 11:9 that they inserted a "not" in "walk in the ways of your heart." The Jewish *Targums* paraphrase 11:9 similarly.

But was Qoheleth contradicting the Pentateuch in 11:9 by advising young people to enjoy themselves and follow the leading of their hearts and eyes? Scholars who argue that there is a blatant contradiction also argue that the warning following that advice in 11:9 was added later for purposes of orthodoxy: "But know that for all these things God will bring you into judgment."

However, no evidence exists to support the theory that Qoheleth was contradicting the Pentateuch. Does not the same hand argue at the end of the book that God will bring every work, every secret deed—much less the leading of your heart and eyes—into judgment to ascertain whether it was good or evil? Consequently, Solomon does not condone a hedonistic Epicureanism or even a relativistic stance that judges the worth of everything by one's own feelings. He urges enjoyment, but likewise cautions that even that rejoicing is reviewable by the God who judges all.

Finally, in linking Ecclesiastes to Scripture that preceded it, we can refer briefly to those wisdom sayings that Ecclesiastes shares with other Scriptures. For example, "He who digs a pit shall fall into it" (10:8) is found in Proverbs 26:27. Another reference in Ecclesiastes, "The dust returns to the earth as it was" (3:20; 12:7), carries the same sentiment as Genesis 3:19*b*: "You are dust, and you will return to the dust" (also Genesis 2:7). Many other echoes of Genesis 1-11 can be listed as follows:

- Man is to live in companionship (Genesis 1:27; Ecclesiastes 4:9-12; 9:9).
- Man is given to sin (Genesis 3:1-6; Ecclesiastes 7:29; 8:11; 9:3).
- Knowledge has God-given limits (Genesis 2:17; Ecclesiastes 8:7; 10:14).
- Life involves tiresome toil (Genesis 3:14-19; Ecclesiastes 1:3; 2:22).
- Death is inevitable for all mankind (Genesis 3:19, 24; Ecclesiastes 9:4-6; 11:8).
- Order and regularity of nature are God's sign of blessing (Genesis 8:21—9:17; Ecclesiastes 3:11-12).
- Life is a "good" gift from God (Genesis 1:10, 12, 18, 21, 25, 31; Ecclesiastes 2:24, 26; 3:12-13; 5:18).

Accordingly, creation theology provides a strong context for the theology of Qoheleth.[20]

Thus we must conclude that Solomon was aware of and consciously writing in the stream of antecedent theology and revelation as found in the books known to the Jews prior to the monarchy. His "cosmopolitan" and "universal" stance was deliberately taken to (1) match the special genre he had decided to use as a medium for his work; (2) gain as wide an audience among the Gentiles as possible; and (3) set a new standard of godliness for potential proselytes and Gentiles in general in a society and culture filled with every form of idolatry, indecency, and injustice known to man.

It should be fairly easy to see why Ecclesiastes was included in the canon of Scripture. There was no doubt that Ecclesiastes, or Qoheleth, was to be included in that canon which the Jews received as inspired (the Mishnah uses the expression to "pollute the hands" to indicate its inspiration). And there was no doubt, according to the evidence of the third century B.C. Greek translation called the Septuagint, the argument of Josephus, the translations of Aquila, Symmachus, and Theodotion in the first two Christian centuries, and the catalog of Melito, bishop of Sardis about A.D. 170, that it belonged to the canon of Old Testament Scripture.

The often repeated charge that the Talmud and Midrashim were ambivalent about Ecclesiastes' place

---

20. Charles Forman, "Koheleth's Use of Genesis," *Journal of Semitic Studies* 5 (1960): 254-63; Walter Zimmerli, "The Place and Limit of Wisdom in the Framework of Old Testament Theology," *Scottish Journal of Theology* 17 (1964): 145-58.

in the canon is an overstatement. If the charge is that there were some serious questions about how to interpret Ecclesiastes, the answer is that the problem was not confined to Qoheleth; consider Song of Solomon, Proverbs, and certain Psalms. Further, those objections were all from the school of Shammai, whose rules of interpretation were hotly contested by the school of Hillel. Shammai was in fact overruled by the seventy elders, and so the Synagogue had settled the issue. What is more, the complaint this school raised that the words of Qoheleth contradict one another was only an apparent difficulty that was resolved just as alleged internal contradictions of the same kind in Proverbs were resolved: by careful exegesis of the text.

THE COMPARISON OF ECCLESIASTES WITH ANCIENT NEAR EASTERN TEXTS

Scholars have repeatedly found some of the roots of the sentiments and advice of Qoheleth in the literature of the Near East. Especially striking, in the minds of many, is a possible parallel between Ecclesiastes 9:7-10 and a section from the "Gilgamesh Epic," tablet X, column III (otherwise known as the "Babylonian Flood Story," from approximately 2000 B.C.).

Gilgamesh, where are you wandering?
You will never find the life you look for.
For when the gods created man,
They let death be his share,
and life they withheld in their own hands.

Gilgamesh, fill your belly—
Be merry day and night,
Let your days be full of joy,

Dance and make music day and night.
Let your garments be fresh,
Wash your head and bathe.
Pay attention to the child holding your hand,
And let your wife delight in your embrace.
These things alone are the task of men[?].
None cometh from thence [i.e., from the place of the dead]
That he may tell us how they fare,
That he may tell us what they need,
That he may set our heart at rest[?],
until we also go to the place whither they are gone.[21]

From a third millennium B.C. Egyptian wisdom text called the "Instruction of Ptahhotep" came this description of old age, the subject Qoheleth pursued in Ecclesiastes 12:3-7:

> Old age hath come and dotage hath descended. The limbs are painful and the state of being old appeareth as something new. Strength hath perished for weariness. The mouth is silent and speaketh not. The eyes are shrunken and the ears deaf----. The heart is forgetful and remembereth not yesterday. The bone, it suffereth in old age, and the nose is stopped up and breatheth not. To stand up and to sit down are alike ill. Good is become evil. Every taste hath perished.[22]

In the first selection above, the young woman, Siduri the winemaker, gives Gilgamesh advice on the goal of

---

21. Author's paraphrase. A translation can be found in H. Frankfort et al., *Before Philosophy* (Harmondsworth, Eng.: Pelican, 1949), p. 226.
22. Adolf Erman, *The Literature of the Ancient Egyptians*, trans. Aylward M. Blackman (1927); reprinted as *The Ancient Egyptians: A Sourcebook of Their Writings*, New York: Harper & Row, 1966), p. 55.

life. But in Ecclesiastes 9:7-10 there is no resignation, as there is in Siduri's advice. Instead Solomon says, "Go on, eat, enjoy your food, and drink your wine with a happy heart, since already God has approved your deed." However, Solomon does not embrace hedonism. Life, whether it be play or work, is subject to current and final reviews by God. Siduri wrongly believed that mankind should only play and that life after death was withheld from all persons; that is hardly the message of Ecclesiastes. Such a morbid prospect can be found elsewhere, for example, in the Egyptian funeral banquet song known as "The Song of the Harpist":

> Be glad. . . . Follow thy desire, so long as thou livest. Put myrrh on thine head, clothe thee in fine linen, and anoint thee. . . . and vex not thine heart,—until that day of lamentation cometh to thee.[23]

In this piece (which is alleged to reflect the sentiments of Ecclesiastes 2:24; 3:12-13; 5:17; 9:7-9; and 11:7-9), the friends of the deceased gathered in the tomb and, surrounded by flowers, wine, a meal, and music, heard this section along with Siduri's theme of the enjoyment of life. Solomon's list is in the form of an allegory and focuses on a somewhat different set of geriatric signs.

The "Instruction of Ptahhotep," quoted above on old age, is fair enough and has some vague similarities to Ecclesiastes 12:3-7. But the "Instruction of Ptahhotep" has another word of advice that is said to be

---

23. Ibid., p. 133.

similar to Ecclesiastes 5:18-19: "Every man also to whom God has given wealth." That word of advice reads:

> Reverence [the man of repute] in accordance with what hath happened unto him, for wealth cometh not of itself. . . . It is God that createth repute. . . . The vestibule [of the great] hath its rule. . . . It is God who assigneth the foremost place.[24]

Obviously, on the basis of these samples, it is clear that Solomon did not borrow any of his materials for Ecclesiastes en bloc from the Egyptians, and they supply the best parallels from the Near East to his book. Neither was he party to their pessimistic views about death.

Surprisingly, Solomon and the Egyptian writers did share many common topics. The light of common grace is evident, especially in the last citation from the "instruction of Ptahhotep," where one's position of eminence in government and wealth both came from God alone. Moreover, from the earliest times the search for the worth, meaning, and goal of life was such a burning issue in the hearts of men that Solomon properly addressed himself to this wider audience of readers on the very perplexity that threatened their existence. But in no way was the final shape of our canonical book of Ecclesiastes affected, as any fair reading of this evidence will demonstrate. The similarities are shared joy for living life and a concern about old age—its disenablements and its regard for

---

24. Ibid., p. 58-59.

wisdom. Solomon was undoubtedly aware of this Egyptian literature, but, as 1 Kings 4:29-32 says, he excelled "all the people of the East and all the wisdom of Egypt"—and that had to be a remarkable feat attributable only to the gift of God.

THE OCCASION FOR READING ECCLESIASTES IN LATER TIMES

One final remark might help to set the tone for us. Ecclesiastes was intended to be a book in celebration of "joy" and God's "good" creation. In Judaism, this book was read on the third day of the Feast of Tabernacles. It is most unlikely, as O. S. Rankin suggested,[25] that this reading was done to bring some sobering thoughts about the brevity and seriousness of life into the midst of all the levity and cheerfulness of that festival. Had not Nehemiah rebuked the people of his day for mixing weeping and mourning with the Feast of Tabernacles (Nehemiah 8:9)? His advice was that they should:

Go on, eat the rich food
and drink sweet wine
and send gifts to those who cannot provide for themselves,
for this day is holy to our Lord;
and do not be sad,
for the joy of the Lord is your strength. (Nehemiah 8:10)

Constantly, Solomon likewise advocated joy and rejoicing, because life is a gift from God. Very few commentators have seen this emphasis on *śimḥah* (joy); among the few who have are Robert Gordis, Edwin

---

25. O. S. Rankin in *The Interpreter's Bible,* ed. George A. Buttrick, 12 vols. (Nashville: Abingdon, 1951-57), 5:4.

Good, Norton Lohfink, and Robert Johnston.[26] In fact, this Hebrew root *simḥah,* meaning "joy, gladness, pleasure," along with the verb *samadohh,* "to be glad, rejoice in," appears seventeen times in Ecclesiastes. Johnston pointed out that in the Old Testament, *samaḥ* may refer to communal jubilation for a festival, a gathering for religious and ritual purposes (see Psalm 45:15), or the individual mood of joy (see Proverbs 14:13.

So, the mood of Ecclesiastesis one of delight, with the prospect of living and enjoying all the goods of life once man has come to fear God and keep His commandments.

Questions for Discussion

1. Read Ecclesiastes 12:8-14. What was the author's intention in writing the book of Ecclesiastes?
2. What two themes emerge in the epilogue? How do those themes relate to the whole of Ecclesiastes?
3. Read Ecclesiastes 3:11. What is the central theme of the book?
4. Examine Dr. Kaiser's structural breakdown of Ecclesiastes. What is the advantage of the fourfold division?
5. What is the significance of the name *Qoheleth?* How is its meaning best interpreted?
6. Who is the author of Ecclesiastes?

---

26. Gordis, p. 131; Edwin Good, *Irony in the Old Testament* (Philadelphia: Westminster, 1965), p. 191; Norton Lohfink, *The Christian Meaning of the Old Testament* (London: Burns & Oates, 1969), pp. 154-55; and Robert Johnston, "[TH] 'Confessions of a Workaholic': A Reappraisal of Qoheleth," *Catholic Biblical Quarterly* 38 (1976): 17-28.

Part 1

Enjoying Life as a Gift from God

Ecclesiastes 1:1—2:26

The writer of Ecclesiastes believed that his book was an argument that came to a conclusion in 12:13-14. Therefore, we can fairly conclude, as was argued in the introductory chapter, that each of his four sections added something to the progress of that argument. Consequently, the best way to begin to analyze the book is to look at the conclusion of the first section in 2:24-26 to determine where the writer, Solomon, believed his first section led him. If we can accurately understand that conclusion, we might then be able to follow with greater certainty the steps leading up to it.

The first section of Ecclesiastes ends by saying:

24. There is not a good [inherent] in man that he should be able to eat, drink, or get satisfaction from his work. Even this, I realized, was from the hand of God.

25. Apart from Him, who can eat and who can have enjoyment?

50 Quality Living

> 26. For to the man who pleases Him, He gives wisdom, knowledge, and joy; but to the sinner He gives the work of gathering and heaping up in order to give it to the one who pleases God. This also is vanity and a chasing after wind.

Two principles are quickly established from these verses:

- The *possession* of the blessings and "goods" of life is a gift from God. All good things must be received and understood as coming from the hand of God if they are to be used properly and joyfully.
- Men and women definitely do not have it within their *ability* to extract enjoyment from life or from any of its most mundane functions, such as eating, drinking, or earning a paycheck. Only God can give that ability to those who come to Him in belief.

This translation of 2:24-26 and the two principles derived from it must, of course, be substantiated by the passage itself. Especially noticeable is the fact that we did not translate verse 24 to say, "There is nothing better"; however, a somewhat similar phrase indicating such a comparison does appear in 3:12 and 8:15. Scholars uniformly assume that a word indicating "better" has dropped out of the Hebrew text of 2:24, because it does appear in the other two passages. But no evidence supports that assumption, even though the translators of most English versions adopted it. They reasoned that the point of Qoheleth is that nothing is left for mankind but to try calmly to enjoy the present. The present is all that is left to man. The best

Enjoying Life as a Gift from God 51

that man can do is to get some physical pleasure out of life while he can. But as Leupold argues,[1] the only translation of verse 24 that is in harmony with verses 25-26 and that properly leads into chapter 3 is: "There is not a good [inherent] in man." There is simply no comparison being made in verse 24. Neither is the preposition in the phrase "There is not a good [inherent] in man" to be equated with a different preposition ("*for*") in 6:12 and 8:15.

Thus we must conclude that even the most mundane and earthly things of life do not lie within man's grasp to donate to himself. The course of all good, contrary to the expectations of most systems of humanism and idealism, cannot be located in man. "He doesn't have it," as the saying goes. It is all beyond him. Rather, it must come from God. Man must get accustomed to realizing that if he is to receive satisfaction from his food and drink, that satisfaction, like all satisfaction, will have to come from the hand of God.

Verse 25 reaffirms the principle that apart from Him, no one is able to eat or enjoy anything. Some versions read "apart from me," that is, as if it spoke of the laborer in the first person: "Who but I should be first to enjoy my labors?" But eight Hebrew manuscripts, the early Greek translation (Septuagint), the Coptic version, the Syriac, and Jerome all read "apart from Him," that is, God. This meaning also fits the context best and is not as awkward as the first person rendering. Thus, the situation is as Delitzsch concluded:

---

1. Herbert C. Leupold, *Exposition of Ecclesiastes* (Columbus, Ohio: Wartburg, 1952), pp. 75-76.

> In enjoyment man is not free, it depends not on his own will: labor and enjoyment of it do not stand in a necessary connection; but enjoyment is a gift which God imparts.[2]

What, then, is the basis on which God distributes His goods and His gift of enjoyment to men? Verse 26 presents that ground. So unexpected is the message of the verse in the eyes of some interpreters that they attribute this verse to a pious writer who added it on his own. How, they ask, can a verse that argues that the good things of life come to those who please God be fitted into the general argument of the rest of the book? This view, they complain, is too cheerful about the state of affairs of life to sit easily with the book's general argument.

But verse 26 merely substantiates the second statement found in verse 24; namely, that the gift of eating and drinking and getting satisfaction from one's work is from the hand of God. The basis of this reward is "pleasing God." The opposite of being a God-pleaser is "one who continues to live in sin." The same contrast between being pleasing to God and being a "sinner" is found in 7:26 and 8:12-13. Those two characters are also carefully defined: a sinner is "one who does not fear God," and thus he is "an evil doer," whereas the man pleasing God will fear Him and do good.

Now to this God-pleaser are granted wisdom,

---

2. Franz Delitzsch, *Commentary on the Song of Songs and Ecclesiastes,* trans. M. G. Easton (1877; reprinted in *Biblical Commentary on the Old Testament,* by C. F. Keil and Franz Delitzsch, Grand Rapids: Eerdmans, 1950), p. 253.

knowledge, and joy as divine gifts. All three are gifts, and joy is last in the order, for it is the real turning point. Previously the writer had viewed wisdom, knowledge, and joy separately and in themselves as possible keys to satisfaction and meaning in life (1:16-17; 2:1). But since they were not received as gifts from God and in the context of "pleasing" Him, that is, fearing and serving Him, he had judged them at that time to be "a chasing of wind" (1:17) and a "vanity" (2:1).

Was "this also . . . vanity and a chasing after wind?" Hardly. In verse 26, the reference is to the frustrating activity of the sinner, who is also divinely given a task. But in his case the task is a troublesome business of gathering and amassing, only to lose it to those who please God. Commentators incorrectly refer "this also is vanity" to the three gifts of "wisdom, knowledge, and joy," but how in anybody's view can God's gifts to men be classified as so much vanity and as elusive as the wind?

Man, for all his empty and vexatious toil in accumulating as much as he can in as brief a time as possible, does so only to see it afterward converted to the uses of good. If only the sinner would come to know God, and if only he would then receive from God the ability to enjoy the possession of all things. In his hopes of finding joy in the security of owning what he has carefully stored up around himself, the final stroke of irony is and always will be that the sinner will be forever cut off from that one possession dearer than all others, joy itself. Solomon's experience is conclusive on this point; few men have exceeded the bounds of his possessions; yet he, too, lacked happiness, wisdom, and knowledge when he began "living in sin." So argues the conclusion to the first section of Ecclesiastes.

The first section, like the three that follow it, contains three subdivisions:

1. 1:4-11   The Restlessness of Life Illustrated
2. 1:12—2:11   The Pleasures of Life Tested
3. 2:12-23   The Purposes of Life Examined

Each subsection builds and prepares for the conclusion in 2:24-26.

After announcing himself in verse 1 (see "Introduction"), Solomon proceeded to the theme in verses 2-3:

2. Vanity of vanities, says Qoheleth,
   Vanity of vanities, all is vanity.
3. What does a man get for all his trouble
   Which troubles him under the sun?

Now we must be careful not to misake the author's use of "vanity" for our own concepts of negativism, futility, and pessimism. Did not Paul utter the same word when he declared in Romans 8:20, "The creation was made subject to vanity," and along with man awaits its final redemption, which is to be found in Christ Jesus our Lord? Theophile Meek reminds us that *hebel*, the Hebrew word for "vanity," takes on different meanings in different contexts—a phenomenon observed in all languages. *Hebel* in 6:12, for example, is best rendered as "empty," says Meek: "For who knows what good there is for man during the few days of his *empty* life, which he spends like a shadow?" In 6:4 it is a "sorry thing": "Though it [the prematurely born] comes as a *sorry thing* and departs in darkness." In 8:14 it is a "senseless thing": "There is a *senseless thing* that takes place on the earth: there are righteous men upon whom comes a fate befitting deeds of the wicked, and there are wicked men upon whom comes a fate befitting deeds of the righteous. I say that this too is *senseless*." "For youth and the prime of life are *transient*."[3]

Thus different aspects of this concept of vanity are used to point to the present state of man and creation now that it has been made subject to "vanity." Interestingly, Paul's (Romans 8:20) Greek term, *mataiots,* is the identical term used in the Septuagint rendering of Qoheleth's *hebel.*

Likewise having a meaning that needs clarification, the "all" in "all is vanity" refers to all the activities of life rather than being a blanket declaration of the total uselessness of the universe. Such a monstrous deduction—that the universe is totally useless—would fly in the face of the repeated conclusion of each of the four sections of this book; namely, that the mundane world is "good" if one realizes that it, too, comes from the hand of God.

When the writer asked rhetorically, "So what is left [*yitron*] for man for all his trouble?" he asked a comparable question to that posed by Jesus in Mark 8:36: "What does it *profit* a man to gain the whole world and yet lose his own soul?" The word for "gain," "profit," or "that which remains or is left over" (*yit-*

---

3. Theophile Meek, "Translating the Hebrew Bible," *Journal of Biblical Literature* 79 (1960): 331.

ron), is drawn from the world of business. J. F. Genung insisted:

> Rather than the word *vanity*, the controlling idea of Koheleth's thought . . . [is] profit. . . . It begins as the plain commercial term denoting the wage or reward. . . . In this everyday application the question is of negative suggestion. But the cosmic setting in which the question here appears creates a broader field of application; making it mean, what surplusage, what overflow of energy or vitality, in life as we see it and live it, what is there left over when it is done?[4]

Genung's observation is correct. Nature and labor both have no residuum, that is, anything left over. There is no benefit, profit, increment, principle of life, or purpose, inherent within nature or labor for man. And that fact weighs heavily on man. But that is jumping ahead of ourselves. Let us turn to each of the three subsections of Ecclesiastes 1-2 to see how Qoheleth itemized his case leading up to his semiclimactic conclusion in 2:24-26.

---

4. John F. Genung, *Words of Koheleth* (New York: Houghton, Mifflin, 1904), pp. 214-15.

2

The Restlessness of Life Illustrated

With a bold hand, Solomon makes his first point in 1:4-11 with four examples from the realm of nature: the earth, sun, wind, and rivers. His concern is pointed: while generations are coming and going, the earth stands. The transitory state of man is strikingly contrasted with the permanently abiding condition of the earth. Now why should this be? Wasn't man made a little lower than the angels? Yet he, not the earth, appears to be in a state of passing away.

Neither does the sun offer any comfort to man, for it continues to rise day after day. Likewise the wind and the rivers maintain their constant motions and uniformity of sequences. Rather than this being an argument for a cyclic view of history, it is instead a composition on the transitoriness of man, who searches nature but finds no fixed point of reference for his own meaning.

Verse 8 concludes that

> All things are restless,
> more than man can say.
> The eye never has enough seeing
> or the ear its fill of hearing.

Thus what was true of the earth, sun, wind, and rivers is also true of all else. The world and its parts could easily be called "the restless ones," ever hastening on, full of labor, weariness, and toil. Such ceaseless activity outstrips the adequacy of any words, the hope of the eyes of ever perceiving it all, and the hunger of the ears to reecho it all.

In all those objects of nature, the fact remains: their existence appears to be permanent and their courses seem regular and uniform, without deviation. Two questions might occur. Doesn't something really new appear from time to time? No, says 1:10, for it has already appeared long ago, before our time. How this could happen is explained in verse 11: man's memory is pretty short. He does not remember the former things, nor will those things that are yet to come be remembered by those who follow later still. Some translators supply the word "generations" with the words "former" and "latter" in the text and thereby argue that the instability and vanishing aspect of man is contrasted with the permanence of nature. Although Ginsburg does not connect verse 11 with its immediate context, verse 10, since he believes that verse 11 refers to verses 2-4, his interpretation nevertheless results in the same point, namely, that man vanishes while nature endures.[1] Consequently "there is no remembrance of former men, nor will there be any remembrance of future men among those who will

---

1. Christian D. Ginsburg, *Coheleth, Commonly Called the Book of Ecclesiastes* [1861; reprinted in *The Song of Songs and Coheleth (Commonly Called the Book of Ecclesiastes)*, The Library of Biblical Studies, edited by Harry M. Orlinsky, New York: Ktav, 1970], pp. 266-67.

live hereafter." For substantiation, he cites 2:16-17 and 9:5. But even if he is correct (and he probably is) in saying that the masculine form of "former" and "latter" demands "men," or "generation," whereas to supply "things" (as Leupold would favor)[2] would demand the feminine form of these words, the idea of this passage and its parallels would still be that no one long remembers the men who lived previously, nor will later generations be any different. The argument does not touch the issue of whether men are immortal. It only speaks of the fickleness of man's memory.

So what is the use then? What do men achieve for all their sweat, worry, and stress? What then is life? Is it merely the dreary rhythm of ceaseless activity? What is left for man for all his trouble? There must be a better answer somewhere else. It cannot reside in these four examples.

Questions for Discussion

1. What two principles may we derive from Ecclesiastes 2:24-26?
2. On what basis does God distribute His goods and gift of enjoyment to men? Why does that basis make a difference?
3. Define *vanity*. For what reasons must we be careful in interpreting its meaning?
4. How is the meaning of the word *profit* best interpreted in the context of Ecclesiastes 1?
5. Read Ecclesiastes 1:4-11. Discuss the examples

---

2. Herbert C. Leupold, *Exposition of Ecclesiastes* (Columbus, Ohio: Wartburg, 1952), p. 49.

Solomon used from the realm of nature. Describe their significance and relation to his conclusion in verse 8.
6. What two questions might we ask that verses 10-11 would answer?
7. Does Solomon's argument provide an answer to the question posed in 1:3? Why?
8. Ecclesiastes 2:24-26 is the conclusion to the first part of the book. How does 1:4-11 contribute to that conclusion?

3

The Pleasures of Life Tested

With the uniformity and permanence of sequences in the natural realm established, as well as the transitoriness and impermanence of the mortal man who is viewing this puzzling contrast, Solomon now turns to speak of his own experience. He will offer his own situation, first in a more general way (1:12-18) and then in more detail (2:1-11).

To begin, 1:12-18 is a sort of double introduction to the book after the question of 1:2-3 has been posed and briefly illustrated in 1:4-11. This double introduction may be divided as Addison G. Wright suggested: (a) 1:12-15, with verse 15 being a proverb to close the unit; (b) 1:16-18, with verse 18 being a proverb to close the unit. Furthermore, Wright believed that there is a partial A-B, B-A form (chiasmus) in these two introductions:

A. "I applied my mind" (v. 13).
B. "I have seen everything" (v. 14).

B. "I have acquired great wisdom . . . my mind has had great experience (vv. 16-17).
A. "I applied my mind" (v. 17).[1]

---

1. Addison G. Wright, "Riddle of the Sphinx: The Structure of the Book of Qoheleth," *Catholic Biblical Quarterly* 30 (1968): 326.

At the least, "I applied my mind" (vv. 13 and 17) is what is known as an inclusion (a sort of bracketing off of material by beginning and ending a section with the same or a similar word or phrase).

Now if Solomon did indeed compose this treatise of Ecclesiastes for a mixed audience of Israelites and Gentiles, who, like the Queen of Sheba, came from afar to sample his wisdom, then his message and example would be adapted to the level of his audience. And if Solomon is going to give advice, he must first state his qualifications for pursuing the proposed inquiry, What advantage is there in this life for man?

Simply stated, his qualifications included:

- He had been ruling as king over Israel in Jerusalem (v. 12).
- He had diligently applied himself to this question (v. 13).
- He had carefully observed all that pertained to this question (v. 14).
- He had acquired more wisdom and knowledge than most other people (v. 16).
- He found much grief and sorrow in things as they were (v. 17).

The careful reader will notice that Qoheleth has now switched from the third person of 1:1-2 ("The words of Qoheleth, the assembler [of the people], son of David, king in Jerusalem") to the first person ("I, the Assembler [of the people], was king in Jerusalem" [1:12]). As we saw in the introduction, 1:12 can easily be translated, "I Qoheleth, *have been* king in Jerusalem" up to this time. If any man could unlock the mysteries in this topic, it would be this famed wise man from Jerusalem.

Solomon plunged enthusiastically into the investigation. He "searched" (from a Hebrew word meaning "to seek the roots of a matter") and "explored" (the Hebrew literally meaning "to investigate a subject on all sides")[2] all things done under heaven. In all candor, he records that he found the task a "sore travail" (ill business *or* sorry task) that God had given to "the sons of the man" (Hebrew has "Adam" or "man," not "men"). Was Solomon thereby alluding to Adam and the effects of the Fall? Yes, he was. He did not choose to say "sons of *men*." The sons of Adam labor and toil without finding any satisfaction or answer to the question. What is the profit? Yet all the time it is God who continues to prompt man's heart to discover the truth. Man is trapped by the difficulty of the problem and his own divinely implanted hunger to know. It is a very tricky business indeed.

From the wealth of his person observation and interviews with men and women of every calling from all sorts of foreign lands, Solomon's conclusion is almost brutal. The "good" and "profit" that any part of this world has to offer is, "All is vanity and a chasing of the wind" (v. 14). Creation has truly been subject to vanity. Size the world up as one may, it still comes out to the same fruitless result.

Verse 15 defines in what sense the conclusion of the preceding verse is to be understood. No investigation,

---

2. George A. Barton, *A Critical and Exegetical Commentary on the Book of Ecclesiastes* (1908; reprinted in The International Critical Commentary, ed. Samuel R. Driver, Alfred Plummer, and Charles A Briggs, Edinburgh: T. & T. Clark, 1959), p. 78.

the concluding proverb of verse 15 says, is going to be able to make up what is deficient and lacking from anything in this world. So much is lacking that it boggles the mind to even try to count it up. Neither can all that is crooked, twisted, perverted, and turned upside down be set right and put in order given merely the materials at hand in this world. However, Solomon's proverb is applied too broadly if he is understood to be claiming that there is no use trying to change anything ever because nothing can ever be straightened out and the deficiencies are too numerous ever to be patched. Rather, the proverb summarizes the fruit of Solomon's search on a horizontal, terrestrial plane. The problem calls for a solution greater than the sum of all its parts.

Once again, as if to introduce the book anew, Solomon repeats in 1:6 his qualifications to conduct the search for an answer to the question of 1:3, What is the use of anything? In pondering the issue, he notes for his reader's appreciation the position from which he answers their plaintive cry. "Look," he says, "I have grown great" in wealth and dignity. Furthermore, "My mind has had great experience in wisdom and knowledge." In an attempt to let contraries explain each other, he pondered folly as well as wisdom.

The result was again put in a proverb in verse 18: Wisdom, when viewed apart from that wisdom which comes from the fear of God—which he eulogizes in 2:13-14 and other verses—increases grief instead of bringing relief to the question of profit. This is proud, human wisdom which says Ginsburg, "Dethrones God and defies man, pretending to give him laws and regulations whereby to make him happy."[3]

After Solomon has completed his list of qualifications to speak to this question in a sort of double introduction, with two proverbs that set forth his results in a general way, in 2:1-11 he elucidates more specifically what proofs and tests he had used to come to his conclusions. Using the form of a monologue (such as can be found in Psalms 42:5, 11; 43:5; or Luke 12:19: "I will say to my soul, soul, thou hast much goods"), Solomon investigated the "profit" of the following areas of life:

- mirth and pleasure (vv. 1-3)
- building and land improvements (vv. 4-6)
- possessions and music (vv. 7-8)

With what hilarity and laughter must the palace halls have echoed as Solomon, his courtiers, and his guests exchanged jokes, drank wine, listened to the witty merrymakers from all over the region, and feasted bountifully *each day* on "thirty measures of fine flour, sixty measures of meal, ten fat oxen, twenty oxen from the pastures, one hundred sheep, in addition to harts, roebucks, fallowdeer and fattened fowl" (1 Kings 4:22-23)! Some estimates suggest that it would take thirty or forty thousand people to consume that much food each day. No wonder 1 Kings

---

3. Christian D. Ginsburg, *Coheleth, Commonly Called the Book of Ecclesiastes* [1861; reprinted in *The Song of Songs and Coheleth (Commonly Called the Book Ecclesiastes)*, The Library of Biblical Studies, ed. Harry M. Orlinsky, New York: Ktav, 1970], p. 275.

4:20 says, "Judah and Israel were as many as the sand which is by the sea in multitude, eating and drinking, and making merry." The whole plan was to sample mirth, pleasure, wine, and folly until he could determine what was "good" for the sons of man (again, sons of Adam?).

Without telling us the results, he passes immediately to an account of his vast building and land improvements. For himself, he devoted thirteen years to building "the king's house" (1 Kings 9:10). Then he built "the house for the forest of Lebanon" (1 Kings 10:17) and another house for his wife, pharaoh's daughter. He also built the cities of Hazor, Megiddo, Gezer, Beth-horon, Baalath, and Tadmor in the wilderness.

Solomon also moved into horticulture, gardening, and the nursery business (2:5-6). In doing so he carried out the original cultural mandate given to man in the garden of Eden: he was to cultivate, work, and guard it. (Note, as Ginsburg pointed out,[4] that the Hebrew word for *vineyard* [*gan*] is from *ganan*, meaning "to guard." So we see that the job of protecting is reflected also in the Germa [*Garten*] and English [*garden*] words for the concept.)

The pools of water used to irrigate his young trees may be the traditional pools of Solomon which are located several miles southwest of Jerusalem in the Valley of Artas. There, according to Robinson (as cited by Ginsburg), "Huge reservoirs built of squared stones and bearing marks of the highest antiquity"

---

4. Ibid., pp. 280-81.

were set in a steep part of the valley. The three pools, measured in feet, had the following sizes:

	Length	Breadth	Depth
Lower	582	207	50
Middle	423	250	39
Upper	380	236	25

To these improvements, Solomon added many possessions (vv. 7-9). An account of Solomon's riches appears in 1 Kings 10:14-29. According to some estimates (taking a talent of gold to be worth approximately fifteen hundred uninflated dollars), his annual income was over one million dollars in purchasing power. Rare and curious things, distinctive to kings and kingdoms, were amassed by Solomon's fleets at Ophir (1 Kings 9:26-28). So great was his fortune that silver and gold were soon to be regarded in Jerusalem as stones (1 Kings 10:27; 2 Chronicles 1:15). In fact, he owned whatever he looked on, and his look went everywhere.

But the worth of all this acquiring and building had to be evaluated. What was the advantage and profit (1:3) of this labor? The answer remained—there was no advantage! Something was sadly missing. Not one of all those good things had brought satisfaction or joy.

Questions for Discussion
1. Describe the structure of Ecclesiastes 1:12-18.
2. Read Ecclesiastes 1:12-17. What qualified Solo-

mon to base his investigation in part on his own experience?
3. What is the theological significance of the phrase *sons of the man?*
4. In which areas of life did Solomon choose to investigate "profit."
5. What was the conclusion of Solomon's investigation? How does it contribute to the larger conclusion of 2:24-26?

4

The Purposes of Life Examined

Now that it was clear that few if any would ever rival the king in possessions and building projects, what could any other man do who followed an act such as this one put on by Solomon? Man's quest for the real profit of life seemed hopeless when the likes of Solomon had had such unprecedented opportunities to test every conceivable benefit to be derived from the goods and projects of this world and had been left unsatisfied. No, the value of life had to lie in other avenues. What about wisdom, madness, and folly?

It became clear (v. 13) that wisdom is vastly superior to any of the acquisitions or pleasures secured from things. The benefit of wisdom over folly is comparable to that of light over darkness. The wise man can see farther ahead and in many directions (his "eyes are in his head" [v. 14]. Yet is this obvious "advantage" (*yitron,* cf. 1:3) a permanent one? Can wisdom also insulate us from the attack of death?

The sad answer is no. One event overtakes both the fool and the wise man—death (v. 15). Both die, and both are forgotten by men (v. 16). Life in itself does not provide such gains as to answer the question of what advantage there is in life. If this is all there is—

the wise man and the fool die alike and are alike forgotten—then life is a cheat and a delusion (v. 17). All the labor spent in acquiring wisdom gives little if any ultimate advantage.

But if wealth and wisdom are both dead-end trails in this search, perhaps there is satisfaction in laying up wealth for others or for one's children. Regrettably, that also is no solution. There is no way of knowing whether that inheritance will be used wisely or foolishly (vv. 18-21).

So Solomon concludes this first section as he began it: "What is there to man" (2:22; "what advantage is there to man?" [1:3]). Day and night he has seen only toil of body and mind. Man does not possess anything within or outside himself to aid him in securing permanent happiness.

Only now are we prepared to receive Solomon's hard-hitting conclusion in 2:24-26:

- There is nothing (inherently) good in man.
- No one can appreciate such elementary things as eating and drinking apart from a personal relationship with the living God.
- God alone—not things or wisdom—is the giver of satisfaction and joy.
- God also gives wisdom, knowledge, and joy for those who please Him.

In contrast to this, how far off the mark is every other pursuit? The question of 1:3, What does life in and of itself profit a man? can now be answered.

The conclusion of 2:24-26: The purpose of life cannot be found in any one of the good things found in the world. All the things that we call the "goods" of life—health, riches, possessions, position, sensual pleasures, honors, and prestige—slip through man's hands unless they are received as a gift from God and until God gives man the ability to enjoy them and obtain satisfaction from them. God gives that ability to those who begin by "fearing," that is, believing, Him. (See discussion of "fear" at 8:12-13.)

Questions for Discussion

1. In examining the purpose of life, what areas did Solomon consider?
2. Why is wisdom not really an advantage?
3. How does Ecclesiastes 2:13-23 contribute to the conclusion in 2:24-26?
4. Examine Dr. Kaiser's list of conclusions in 2:24-26. What answer do we have for the question, What does life in and of itself profit a man?

Part 2

Understanding the All-Encompassing Plan of God

Ecclesiastes 3:1—5:20

Solomon's personal experience and the restlessness of nature laid the groundwork for the inescapable conclusion that enjoyment and happiness, if they are ever going to be within man's reach, must come as direct gifts from God to men of faith. The wicked, meanwhile, are left with the aggravating and empty task of accumulating goods that could soon be converted to the uses of those fearing God.

In the next step in his fourfold argument, Solomon boldly argues the thesis that every action of man can be traced to its ultimate source, an all-embracing plan that is administered by God (3:1). This is a beautiful plan, yet men and women do not and, as a matter of fact, cannot apprehend it because of their prevailing worldliness. So vast, so eternal, and so comprehensive in its inclusions is this plan that man is both threatened and exasperated in his attempts to discover it for himself. Nevertheless, being built by God and made in His own image, man possesses a hunger within his heart to know the vastness and eternity of this plan. Yet he cannot know it until he comes to personally know the living God (3:11). Therefore, he is once again cut off from that very substance for which his whole being yearns, just as he likewise searched for happiness and joy in chapters 1 and 2.

The structure of Solomon's argument in this section is precisely what it was in the first section:

1. 3:1-15: The Principle: God has a plan that embraces every man and woman and all their actions in all times.
2. 3:16—4:16: The Facts: The anomalies and apparent contradictions in this thesis are examined and reflected upon.
3. 5:1-17: The Implications: Certain cautions and warnings must be raised lest a hasty calculation lead men and women to deny the reality and existence of God's providence and plan.
   Conclusion: 5:18-20.

Once again, it will be best to start with the writer's conclusion to the section as we attempt to assess the development of the principle that God has an all-embracing plan that covers all men, times, and actions. Thus we propose to judge the whole section of 3:1—5:17 in light of its intended goal in 5:18-20. The following list is a fair appraisal of the writer's conclusion to the second part of his work.

- God's proposed course of living is "good," that is, without moral problems (v. 18*a*).

- God's plan can also be declared to be a "very fine," or "beautiful," path to tread. It possesses aesthetic and practical qualities, along with its moral perfections (v. 18b).
- Enjoyment, not worldly accumulations, is the principal end to be sought. Therefore, neither the plan of God nor religion was ever meant to stifle our pleasure and joy in possessing things or in life itself (v. 18c).
- In fact, the man who has learned the secret of enjoyment as a gift from God will not become anxious over the length of his life. He has too much joy in living to brood over the impermanence of his mortal being. Rather, each day is taken as it comes, as a gift from God (vv. 18d-19).
- God himself "answers" (v. 20b), that is, makes His person to correspond to the joy in man's heart. Men are thereby kept occupied and delighted in the inner recesses of their lives with God Himself. Consequently, the dark side of man's brief life is relieved and exchanged for gladness in the plan of God.

Thus we arrive at the same conclusion as that given in 2:24-26, with the addition that the scheme, or the plan, of life itself is not monotonous or dreary because it, too, is in the hands of God. Why then should man brood, sulk, and curse any aspect of God's gift of life or His promised ability to enjoy everything, no matter how trivial, mundane, or ephemeral in comparison to Himself? But let us turn now to the development of the argument.

5

God's All-Encompassing Plan

For all the affairs of life, argues Qoheleth, God has set a time. The length of time and the particular events along that time band are each ordained in the providence of God.

To illustrate this broad and comforting assertion, the writer turns to fourteen pairs of opposites in verses 2-8. Twenty-eight times, "time" is repeated as he presses home the point of God's foreordination and man's accountability.

Some (e.g., Leupold)[1] have attempted to interpret these pairs of contrasting events as if they were intended to signify the church or the nations. The result is a travesty of the meaning intended by the author. It simply cannot be shown that Qoheleth meant by the idea of birth to signify moral regeneration; by death, the death of the old, sinful nature of man; by planting, the spiritual implantation of truth in the heart; by uprooting, the destruction of the sin principle in the heart of man; by killing, the mortification of sin; by healing, the recovery from sin; and so on. Nor was the writer limiting or directing his remarks to the birth

---

1. Herbert C. Leupold, *Exposition of Ecclesiastes* (Columbus, Ohio: Wartburg, 1952), p. 82.

God's All Encompassing Plan   77

and death of nations per se. (Compare, however, Jeremiah 1:10 for the pairs to "plant, uproot" and "build, tear down.")

The references in verses 2-8 are basically to individuals. The plan of God encompasses everything from our being born to the day of our death. God appoints both our birthday and the day of our funeral. Thus the entirety of human existence begins the list of fourteen illustrations of the comprehensiveness of the plan of God.

Next Qoheleth moves to the vegetable realm and teaches us that even the life of vegetables is set in the scope of God's plan—when they are to be planted and when they are to be harvested (v. 2). (It may be noted in passing that this pair is also used later in Jeremiah 18:7 and Zephaniah 2:4, among other references, to apply metaphorically to nations.)

Having established that the term of life if fixed for men as well as for the plant world, Solomon teaches that even those situations that seem to be in the hands of men and, therefore, somewhat unpredictable—such as the condemnation of murderers by the state to the penalty of death—are likewise embraced in the plan of God. There is a time for executing murderers or destroying enemies in a just war (v. 3). (Incidentally, such action against murderers is favored in Scripture, not because men are sovereign or because society and the bereaved are somehow benefited, but because man is so vastly important to God—he is made in the image of God [Genesis 9:6]. To kill another person is to kill God in effigy. Thus the only alternative that the state, God's duly authorized agent in such a case, has is to show respect for God and for the value of the image of God in man by taking the murderer's life. Such a moral reason has not been antiquated by any subsequent revelation in the gospel. And how could it be antiquated? Can the character of God be offered at discount value in generations to come?) Along with taking life in those designated times, the plan of God includes a time "to heal," or, literally, "to sew," "to heal a wound." Likewise, there is a time to break down old walls, relationships, or even, metaphorically, nations (e.g., Jeremiah 18:7, 9), as well as a time to build them up.

Intimately connected with these examples of the antithesis in God's providence are the sorrows and joys that accompany the events described in verses 2-3. Solomon begins in verse 4 with "to weep" (*libkot*), possibly because it (the Hebrew word) sounds so similar to the last word in the preceding set, *libnot* (to build). So also "to leap, dance" ($r^e eqod$) is probably used instead of "to rejoice" ($s^e emoah$) because it sounds like "to mourn" ($s^e epod$).[2] Accordingly, divine providence warrants times of laughter, joy, and pleasure.

This list of attitudes is continued in verse 5, where what was once easily discarded as so many useless stones would on another occasion be earnestly sought out as valuable building materials. Thus men often treat one and the same material or person differently depending on their condition, needs, and the control-

---

2. Christian D. Ginsburg, *Coheleth, Commonly Called the Book of Ecclesiastes* [1861; reprinted in *The Song of Songs and Coheleth (Commonly Called the Book of Ecclesiastes)*, The Library of Biblical Studies, ed. Harry M. Orlinsky, New York: Ktav, 1970], p. 305.

ling power of God. Put in proverbial terms, there is a time to embrace (the familiar) and a time to refrain from embracing.

So much for the usual, the common, the familiar in all its forms; but the same thing can be said for man's desire to get new things. There are times (v. 6) when he should seek new objects, even though there will be other times when he will lose some of those earthly treasures. Likewise, along with the acquisition of new properties, there are times for guarding things and times for throwing them away. For example, in verse 7 Solomon applied this contrast to the abandoning and preserving of clothing. When bad news came, it was appropriate in Solomon's time to rip the front of one's garment to display one's grief (2 Samuel 13:31); with the passing of the problem, it was proper to sew the torn clothes together again.

But what of the great calamities of life? Here again, there are times when it is best to remain silent in the heart of adversity (2 Kings 2:3, 5), and there are times when one has to speak and cry out, even if to no one else but God (v. 7). Men are placed in situations in which they are stirred to love or moved to hate. In Psalm 105:25 God "turned" the "hearts" of the Egyptians "to hate" and "to deal craftily" with Israel, whereas Israel enjoyed favor from that same nation under the good hand of God as they asked for jewels (Exodus 11:3). So Solomon concluded the series with the message that there are divinely appointed times for war and peace (v. 8).

Yet the question persisted: What is to be gained from the whole scene? Ecclesiastes 3:9 is but a return to the question of 1:3. The answer is clear. All life unfolds under the appointment of Providence—birth, death; growth, harvest; joys, sorrows; acquiring, losing; speaking up, being silent; war and peace. Since everything has its time from God, all the labor of man by itself cannot change the times, circumstances, or control of events.

But 3:10 must be taken together with verse 11. For upon further revelation, it must be boldly announced that God has made all the events and relationships in life "beautiful." And in addition to the beauty of this order of things, He has also implanted in the hearts of men a desire to know how this plan of God makes all the details fit together.

Everything, as it came from the hand of the Creator in Genesis 1, was "very good." Even the activities of verses 2-8, which in themselves do not appear beautiful, have a beauty when they are seen as constituent parts of the whole work of God. In God's world plan, He "had made" all things to fit in their appointed time and place (v. 11). So integrated is this total work of God that man, likewise a creation of God, yearns in the depths of his being to trace the providential dealings of God's government from beginning to the end; yet he cannot.

The key word in 3:11 is "eternity": "God has put *eternity* into their heart." This quest is a deep-seated desire, a compulsive drive, because man is made in the image of God to appreciate the beauty of creation (on an aesthetic level); to know the character, composition, and meaning of the world (on an academic and philosophical level); and to discern its purpose and destiny (on a theological level). There is the majesty and madness of the whole thing. Man has an inborn inquisitiveness and capacity to learn how everything in his experience can be integrated to make a whole. He wants to know how the mundane "downstairs" realm of ordinary, day-to-day living fits with the "upstairs" realm of the hereafter; how the business of living, eating, working, and enjoying can be made to fit with the call to worship, serve, and love the living God; and how one can accomplish the integration of the natural sciences, social sciences, and humanities. But in all the vastness and confusion, man is frustrated by the "vanity" of selecting any one of the many facets of God's "good" world as that part of life to which he will totally give himself.

Here again, man first has to come to terms with the living God. Life and its "goods" are gifts from the hands of the living God (vv. 13-15). Life will remain an enigma and a frustration until men come to "fear," that is, to believe, the God who made man and the goods and truths of His world. (See below for discussion of "the fear of God.") God's work and plan remain intact (v. 14). Just as man cannot, on his own, determine one end from the other (v. 11), so also he cannot add anything to God's plan or take anything from it (v. 14).

Why then does God allow such a great burden of worries, cares, frustrations, and labors to fall on man's shoulders if He can give (1) mundane gifts, (2) the ability to enjoy those gifts, and (3) some knowledge of the all-encompassing plan of God? The answer is, "In order that they should fear before Him" (v. 14). Obedience to the first commandment (Exodus 20:3) must come prior to receiving each of the above three requests; He must be Lord and God above all. Men must begin living by trusting nothing to their own abilities, devices, wisdom, or connections. "It is not," as Paul summarized in Romans 9:16, "to the one that wills [it], nor to one that runs, but to God who shows mercy."

The "fear of God" (3:14) appears in Ecclesiastes at several crucial points (see ·5:7; 7:18; 8:12-13 [three times]; 12:13). This fear is not an attitude of terror. It is instead a commitment of the total being to trust and believe the living God. The preposition that accompanies the expression in 3:14 is forceful in supporting this view—"from *before* Him" (cf. 8:12, emphasis added) The absolute lordship of God in this expression is supported in the parallel invitation for all the nations to come and worship God and "fear before him," for "the Lord reigns" over the whole earth (cf. 1 Chronicles 16:30; Psalm 96:9). The one who fears God dreads nothing more than God's disfavor. Such a worshiper wants nothing more than to know the living God intimately and submit to His will. And God Himself wants to be known and obeyed by man; accordingly, He has shut man up to the enigma of life, yet given him an unquenchable hunger to know how it all, from the simplest to the most profound, fits with everything else.

God's purposes and plan are unchangeable (v. 15). When the text says that God "calls back" or "seeks out" that which is "chased away," it refers either to those who are persecuted (as argued by Luther, Rashi, and the Midrash) or to time itself, which from a human point of view had been lost, but which in God's wise arrangement of events became available for God to bring forward as a part of His wise plan or as a

God's All Encompassing Plan 83

witness at the last judgment. God, then, can call back the past and connect it with the future. With the hint of the divine evaluation in the future of the past deeds of men, we are prepared for the next section.

Questions for Discussion

1. Read Ecclesiastes 3:1—5:20. What is the thesis of Solomon's fourfold argument?
2. Study Dr. Kaiser's list of conclusions derived from Ecclesiastes 5:18-20. How would you sum up those conclusions?
3. Examine the fourteen pairs of opposites. What do they teach us?
4. In light of Solomon's argument, how are we to view the great calamities of life?
5. Read Ecclesiastes 3:11. Explain the significance of the statement "God has put eternity into the heart."
6. Describe the "fear of God" in Ecclesiastes 3:14. What does it mean for us to exercise it?
7. How does Ecclesiastes 3:1-15 support the conclusion in 5:18-20?

6

God's Plan Examined

Six facts are brought forward by Solomon that might tend to negate the thesis God has a plan in operation involving every person and every event:

1. 3:16-17: There is unrighteousness in the halls of justice.
2. 3:18-21: Men and beasts alike die.
3. 4:1-3: Men are oppressed.
4. 4:4-6: Men are rivalrous.
5. 4:7-12: Men are isolated.
6. 4:13-16: Popularity is temporary.

In each of these six cases, the argument is introduced by the phrase "Moreover I saw" (3:16), "I indeed saw" (3:18; 4:4), or "again I saw" (4:1; 4:7); only 4:13 does not use some form of this introduction.

1. So grievous an exception to the overall plan of a good God is unrighteousness in the halls of government that Solomon immediately appended the words of verse 17 as an answer to the charge of verse 16. God instituted human tribunals as places where men could expect to find judicial relief. But when wickedness is offered where justice should be found, that is a matter of utmost seriousness. Such inequities God

God's Plan Examined 85

Himself will rectify in the future judgment, although they appear temporarily to run unabated. Wronging the innocent and clearing the guilty is dangerous business, for all who practice such crookedness and demagoguery will face the Judge of all judges in that final judgment.

2. Although nothing is so prominent at times as the savage way men tyrannize one another in and out of court, death ultimately catches up with all men. But there is the seeming unfairness of it all. Death is the greater leveler of all living beings. It happens to men as it happens to beasts.

Yet by this very same fact, God shows men their frailty in an effort to force them to turn back and search for Himself, to come to the realization that all goods are from His hand, to receive from His hand the ability to enjoy those gifts, and to come to appreciate His plan.

Tragically, we seldom take heart as we ought to the reality of death. We moderns are more primitive in our estimate of and regard for the life hereafter than were the men of antiquity. We are insulated from directly facing the grim aspects of death day in and day out; it was not so with them. They had no gadgetry to occupy their minds, no gracious living to cause them to forget, no hospital and rest homes to remove the smell, sound, and sight of death from them.

Most people conclude that since "all go to one place" (v. 20), that is, the grave (here the idea is not hell), that is the end of it. Certainly, both men and beasts are made out of dust, and their bodies return to the dust; but what poor gamblers men are if they believe that is the end. Verse 21 deliberately adds in the clearest tones possible (despite very little help from some translations), "The spirit of man goes upward, but the spirit of the beast goes down to the earth." (The verbs "to go upward" and "to go downward" are active participles with the article attached to them and not, as some incorrectly insist, the Hebrew sign of the interrogative. The presence of the long "a" in *ha* instead of the short "a" shows that the Hebrew scribes called the Masoretes did not regard verse 21 as an interrogative or conditional sentence.) Had not Solomon already argued that unjust judges will face the living God in the last judgment (3:17)? And will he not with consistency press the same facts into service in 12:7: "The dust returns to the earth as it was, and the spirit returns to God who gave it." What would be the point of concluding his book with the ominous warning that "God will bring every deed into judgment" (12:14) if men are dead and gone? If that is the case, who cares if God reprimands our worms? Neither they nor our dust will much care. But such is not Solomon's thought.

Concepts of man's immortality are as old as Enoch; his body entered the eternal state directly. Even patriarchal Job knew that death is not the end of life. He observed that if you chop down a tree, it often sends out new shoots from the old stump (Job 14:7). Likewise, he contested, if you chop down man so that he dies, there is hope for him also to "shoot" again in new life (Job 14:14; the same root word as in verse 7 is used here, although the fact is obscured in the translations).

If it is argued that verse 21 must be a question

because it begins with "who knows," Leupold[1] convincingly protests that in the nine passages where this expression appears in the Hebrew Bible, only three are followed by the interrogative (Esther 4:14; Ecclesiastes 2:19; 6:12). In another three cases, "Who knows" is followed by a direct object (Psalm 90:11; Ecclesiastes 3:21; 8:1); three more times it is followed either by the imperfect verb or it is a kind of afterthought and means something like "perhaps" (Proverbs 24:24; Joel 2:4; Jonah 3:9). Only the context will decide if the Hebrew phrase is interrogative. Here it calls for a direct object and not a nonchalant remark that no one is actually able to tell the difference between the fates of men and animals.

Men and beasts, then, do differ. Man may be like the beasts in one way—his frail body may return to the dust. But his spirit goes upward to God; whether for judgment or some more pleasant prospect, the writer does not pause at this point to say.

In the meantime, God has something that men may inherit: their portion, if they meet the previously stated conditions of belief, may be to enjoy their work in this life (v. 22). The rhetorical question "Who can bring him to appreciate what will be after him?" is again not answered at this point, but the context is abundantly clear, as is the conclusion to Ecclesiastes: it is God who will in the future evaluate life in its totality.

3. Another complaint emerges to threaten the beau-

---

[1] Herbert C. Leupold, *Exposition of Ecclesiastes* (Columbus, Ohio: Wartburg, 1952), p. 99.

ty of the plan of God—oppression (4:1-3). What a list of possible injuries can be done to person, property, and a person's good name by rulers, masters, fathers, husbands, or any others in positions of responsibility. Theirs is the power. The lot of the oppressed often is the absence of any "comforter" (v. 1). To be without a comforter is worse than death itself (v. 2). Like Jonah (Jonah 4:3) and Elijah (1 Kings 19:4), the oppressed cry, "Lord, take away my life, for it is better for me to die than to live." In fact, so powerfully wrong and so solitary does the case of the oppressed appear, that, like Job (Job 3:3-10), nonexistence is preferred over existence (v. 3). Our mourner will not recover until he, like the psalmist Asaph (Psalm 73:17), goes into the house of God (Ecclesiastes 5:1-6).

4. To the previous three obstacles to acceptance of the rule that God's plan encompasses everything is now added the observation that men can be as cruel and inhuman to each other in unnecessary competition as they can be in oppression (4:4-6). Often the rule of the business world is the law of the jungle. Every success is greeted with envy instead of the expected praise. "Every right work," or "every successful undertaking" (v. 4), is received as Cain greeted Abel's goodness, or as Saul failed to rejoice for David's sake.

It might appear justifiable to just plain forget it all. Why should anyone want to work so hard in a dog-eat-dog world, only to be envied as the reward for his success? Yet Qoheleth warns that such an attitude must not be an excuse for laziness. And to seal that logic, he adds a proverb (v. 5) against the idleness of the fool who folds his hands and comes to ruin, for he figuratively "eats his own flesh" as he consumes what substance he had stored up.

Instead of cruel competitiveness, Solomon recommends moderation. Verse 6 is almost the Pauline injunction. "Godliness with contentment is great gain" (1 Timothy 6:6); or even the Solomonic proverbs: "Better is a little with the fear of the Lord" (Proverbs 15:16, cf. v. 17) and "Better is little with righteousness than great treasures with injustice" (Proverbs 16:8).

5. There are more problems for theodicy. What about the sadness of isolation and solitariness (4:7-12)? Escape from competition may be a temporary solution, because then one has to cope with loneliness. This is a situation in which there is no family left, not even an heir for whom one could work and deprive himself of pleasure. No comforter (4:1-3), no rest (4:4-6), and now no companion (4:7-12): What can be said to this?

Solomon had a proverb for this situation as well: "Two are better than one" (v. 9). Society, not the solitary life, and perhaps marriage, not the single life of celibacy, are to be preferred. For in such intimacy and shared life there is assistance (v. 10), comfort (v. 11), and defense (v. 12). In each of the proverbs of verses 9-12, the advantages of cooperation and companionship are emphasized. In fact, if two are better than one, three friends provide even greater comradeship (v. 12*b*).

6. With a slight variation in the order of things, the proverbial answer comes first (v. 13), whereas the sixth and final obstacle comes last in 4:14-16. How fleeting and altogether temporary is the popularity accorded men. What does it matter if a man even has

royal power? In one case, the old king, although born to the throne, becomes foolish, senile, and unable to discern that his days of ruling are over. In another situation, a young but poor wise man may, like Joseph, rise from prison to the throne. Such are the constant ups and downs of life, for although the young man was welcomed at first (v. 15), he, too, will no doubt share his predecessor's fate: "Those who come later will not be pleased with him" (v. 16). How fickle people are! Today's hero is tomorrow's bum. While rulers tremble and diligently seek to make their thrones secure, the people clamor for change and revolution. Now how can the plan of God encompass the likes of that?

Questions for Discussion

1. Read Ecclesiastes 3:16—4:16. List the six facts Solomon brought forward in the argument against the thesis that God has a plan. How does each contradict the plan of God?
2. Discuss each of the six cases. How do they contribute to the conclusion of 5:18-20?

7

Warnings Against Denying God's Plan

Obstacles there are to believing in God's omnipotence, but none of them should be used as an excuse for neglecting one's relationship to the God who said He is actively in charge of all things. Some people are bound to reflect on the six charges of 3:16—4:16 or even additional anomalies, and be led to practical atheism; that is, they are tempted to act as if God were not in control. Do not be seduced by the six facts discussed above to adopt an irreligious stance to life, begged Qoheleth. Above all else, do "go to the house of God" (5:1) with a receptive attitude and a readiness to listen rather than lecture God on what He ought to do. Worship is here called "sacrifice" because it is offering to God "the calves of our lips" (cf. Hosea 14:2; Hebrews 13:15).

Neither should men attempt to bribe God with vows. How frivolous and unbecoming can mere mortals act? "God is in heaven and [we] are on earth" (5:2), Solomon reminds us. Therefore, our words should be few. And thereby, we are rebuked for all pretense, hypocrisy, and superficial religiosity that hopes to be heard for its "much speaking." Limits are imposed only on the petitioner's pretense, and not on the length of his prayers. There may be times when a person's importunity demonstrates the value and importance of what he asks from God, even as Jacob refused to let the Angel of the Lord go until He blessed him (Genesis 32:26). On the other hand, only fools babble on relentlessly, like a man who has had a busy day and experiences dream after dream all night long (v. 3).

But when vows are made to God, they must be carried out (v. 5). Ananias and Sapphira lied and experienced the judgment of God (Acts 5:1-11). It would have been better had they never vowed at all, or even if they had promised only a part of their land; but they had decided to toy with God in the hopes of gaining greater esteem among the believers of the early church.

The application of verses 6-7 is clear: do not sin with your mouth and do not protest to God's minister (the Hebrew word literally meaning "angel"; cf. Haggai 1:13 and Malachi 2:7, where "angel" means "priest," or "minister," for the Lord). Accordingly, we must watch our mouths when we contemplate such obstacles to faith and enigmas as life produces. Men must learn that their first order of business is to fear God. True piety is the only remedy for every temptation offered us to spew out a sally of empty words against God's good operation of all things. This conclusion agrees with 12:13. Man must begin as a believer and worshiper if he is ever to enjoy living as God intended him to live.

Having established his dominant theme, the fear of God as man's number one priority, Solomon now turns to some of the cases he had previously introduced. His work moves more and more in the direction of a theodicy, that is, an explanation and justification of the ways of God to men.

For the problem of the perversion of justice (see 3:16-18), Qoheleth appeals in 5:8 to the fact that there remains a tribunal that is higher than those who perpetrate those wrongs. It is the tribunal of God. Some have choked on the word "province" (Hebrew *medinah*) and argued that the word was unknown in Israel during Solomon's time. But it must be remembered that Solomon was acquainted with many languages because of his many contacts with the nations of the world. Thus it is natural that he would use a word for a district found outside of Israel at that time. Nevertheless, let no one be surprised, the highest judge of all is the One who will evaluate every judgment ever made.

Verse 9 continues in the same vein of thought. Good government by a delegated officer is a great blessing to any country. This is one source of correction of some of the abuses witnessed by men. Happy indeed is that country that recognizes that the "profit" of the land is for all; ruler and people are happiest when they both realize that they are served by the farmed fields. But should human government also fail, there is still redress from God.

As for the other problems previously raised, Solomon summarizes his case in 5:10-17. It is a case for the unsatisfactory nature of wealth and labor in and of themselves. There is little if any "benefit" in riches per se, he says. Consider that:

- Human desire outruns acquisitions, no matter how large the acquisitions may be (v. 10).

- An increase in wealth demands a corresponding increase in staff to manage it. Wealth seems to attract all sorts of parasites (v. 11).
- Labor may bring sleep, but wealth brings sleeplessness and the fear that a blunder may result in the loss of everything (v. 12).
- Possession is so uncertain and so brief, for often by some accident of speculation (evil travail *or* misfortune, v. 14) the estate dwindles to nothing.
- Last of all, the wealthy man himself must return to his Maker devoid of all his riches, not even having a cloak (vv. 13-16). Nevertheless, there still are men who will spend all their days in great sorrow and distressing labor for such an empty goal as this (v. 17).

The conclusion remains the same (5:18-20). Man must get enjoyment, not possessions. And that capacity to enjoy, no matter how great or how small, is a gift from God. It is much better to receive wealth as a gift from God, along with the God-given ability to enjoy it, than to see wealth as an end in itself. The condition for the reception of his gift is the same as it was in 2:26, and therefore it is not repeated. How sad that men can spend all their days working and sweating to receive the enjoyment that God offers as a gift if men will seek it in the manner that He, in His excellent and beautiful plan, has chosen to give it. Happiness, enjoyment, pleasure, and a knowledge of how the whole substance of life is integrated into a meaningful pattern in the plan of God are all linked in the living God. To know the "eternity" of all things is, if we may rephrase John 17:3, "to know Him."

Warnings Against Denying God's Plan 95

Questions for Discussion

1. Read Ecclesiastes 5:1-17. How does Solomon answer the six cases discussed in 3:16—4:16?
2. Define a *vow.* How should we view vows made to God?
3. Examine Solomon's summary of his case in Ecclesiastes 5:10-17. Discuss Dr. Kaiser's list of items concerning the "benefits" of riches.
4. What is Solomon's conclusion in Ecclesiastes 5:18-20? How does John 17:3 concur with that passage?

Part 3

Explaining and Applying the Plan of God

Ecclesiastes 6:1—8:15

Qoheleth has shown that enjoyment as a gift from God is preferable to accumulating ever so many possessions, and he has shown that the acquisition of those things, along with all other events in this life, is regulated by a magnificent and beautiful plan.

The next portion in 6:1—8:15 is the central portion of the whole argument. Here Solomon will apply the two conclusions of the first two sections of his work (about the gifts and the plan of God) to the alleged inequalities and the apparently unfair variations in divine providence.

As in the preceding sections, this one easily divides itself into three divisions:

1. 6:1-7:15: Proper evaluation of man's outward fortunes help to explain the apparent inequalities in divine providence.
2. 7:16-29: Proper evaluation of a man's character

helps to explain the apparent inequalities in divine providence.
3. 8:1-14: The removal of a large proportion of the apparent inequalities in divine providence comes from righteous government.

Conclusion: 8:15.

As we have done in previous chapters, let us begin this stage of Solomon's argument by examining his conclusion first. Ecclesiastes 8:15 employs what has become by now the standard formula. God commends enjoyment as one of His most excellent gifts to the men and women who fulfill the previously mentioned condition of fearing Him. And this gift of enjoyment, including eating, drinking, and receiving the joy of living in the favor of God, *will* (not *should*, as some versions translate it, for it is a Hebrew indicative and not a jussive) stay with them. The gifts of God are not dangled on a string before men's eyes, only to be retracted just as they seem to come within reach. The promise is that in the good plan of God, they will accompany men who fear Him. God really intended that men should come to a proper enjoyment of the good material gifts placed in this world by Him, and that the gifts should be a source of constant satisfaction when the things and the users are properly related to the Giver Himself. Such enjoyment is meant to accompany man all the days of his earthly life. The reception of those gifts and the confident contentment in the provision of God are to be preferred over all the restless activity of men, which is devoted solely to accumulating things and using wicked methods to obtain them. No God-fearer ought ever, nor does he ever need, to stoop to low means and obtain nothing but anxiety, sweat, and emptiness as a reward for all his work. Enjoyment is still in the hands of man's Creator and Redeemer.

8

Evaluating Man's Outward Fortunes

Solomon says that a proper evaluation of a man's outward fortunes helps to explain the apparent inequalities in divine providence, an assertion that is developed in two complementary arguments that form two subdivisions of 6:1-7:15:

1. Prosperity is not always or necessarily good (6:1-12).
2. Adversity, or affliction, is not always or necessarily evil (7:1-15).

Let us see how each argument is developed so that we can come to a proper estimate of the fairness and goodness of the plan of God when viewed against the realities of man's *outward* fortunes.

1. "Never judge a book by its cover," goes the old saying, and men should never get confused about the true state of others' affairs by looking merely at their outward welfare. A man may possess wealth, honor, numerous children, long life, and virtually every outward good that anyone could possibly imagine; yet he can still be a very broken, dissatisfied, and unhappy person.

Indeed, this is a weight that weighs heavily on men

(6:1): God may grant a man wealth, possessions, honor, and virtually anything his heart wants without also granting him the ability to enjoy any of it (6:2)! Therein lies the point of Solomon: things are not always what they seem to be. Prosperity without the divine gift of enjoyment is nothing. In fact, God-given wealth without the God-given power to enjoy it is a major malady. Worst of all is that a stranger, not even his own kin, consumes the whole estate from which a man had only joylessly partaken portions.

So immense is this deprivation of enjoyment that even if the case just mentioned were reversed and, instead of his being childless and leaving his possessions to a total stranger, that same man were blessed with an abundance of children; and if, instead of departing from this earthly scene quickly and letting a stranger receive a bonanza of goods, he lived for an unusually long number of days; still, if he were not given the divine gift of enjoying it all, death at birth would have been preferable to what had happened to such a man (6:3). A stillborn baby is free from all the suffering of the joyless rich man and has more rest than he does (6:4-5).

After all the concessions made in verses 3-5, we see that even if an inordinate number of days were offered to this man, they must come to an end. Then he, too, must go to the same place as the stillborn child (6:6). That "one place" is, as seen in 3:20, the grave. What then? If even the longest life eventually terminates having yielded no enjoyment, not to mention any prospect of anything to follow, what is the benefit, or advantage, of all those years? Although others may have looked on with envious eyes, the truth is that the extension was not what it appeared to be; it was a compounded sorrow.

Whereas the man's labor was continually aimed at his insatiable desire for pleasure, he never arrived (6:7). No man, be he wise, poor, or rich, can satisfy his desires on his own (6:8). True, making do with what we possess is better than striving for what we do not have, for all the wishing for things we want is worthless (6:9).

The reason riches fail to yield any happiness rests on the unalterable ordinance of God (v. 10). Mortal man, the creation of God, cannot set aside or overcome that divinely established connection between earthly things and the dissatisfaction with those things apart from knowing God. Try as man will to wrestle and contest God's decision to link these things—the more he talks, the more vapid, empty, and unsatisfactory the situation becomes (6:11). All words are useless; man might just as well acknowledge his limitations and begin immediately to fear God. The ordinance of God dictates the incapacity of worldly things to yield enjoyment; in fact, it must be observed that often worldly prosperity only increases the emptiness and dissatisfaction. We might ask, in the words of Paul in Romans 9:20, "Who art thou, O man, to talk back to God?" Do you know "what is good for man?" (6:12). Does any man know what the future holds? Of course, no one knows except God. Therefore, no one can say what will be the real advantage of one thing or another for himself or others.

If every one of the above cases has shown the inadequacy of judging the fairness and goodness of the plan of God by observing only the external features, then the providence of God may not have so many exceptions as we may have thought as we began to apply the truth of 3:1—that there is a time and season for everything under heaven—especially when compared to the apparent success of the wicked. Prosperity may not always be what it seems. Therefore, let us seek to know God, to be content with such gifts as He gives us, and to receive the accompanying gift of enjoyment from His hands.

2. The companion truth to 6:1-12 is now set forth in 7:1-15: suffering and adversity are not necessarily signs of God's disfavor. In fact, adversity often is a greater good than prosperity!

The question has been posed in 6:12, "What is good?" This becomes the hook on which a series of proverbs giving us some "good" or "better" things is hung. Here are some "good" or "better" things that will prove to be more salutary than prosperity:

- A good name is better than expensive perfume (7:1*a*).
- The day of death is better than the day of birth with its promise of prosperity (7:1*b*).
- Mourning is better than festivity and mirth (7:2).
- Sorrow is better than laughter (7:3).
- Rebuke from a wise man is better than the praise of fools (7:5).
- The end of a thing is better than its beginning (7:8).
- Patience in waiting for God's timing is better than fretting over the elusiveness of things (7:8-9).
- Further affliction may be better than any immediate outward good (7:10-12).

The scenes of sadness in 7:1-6 set the stage for the argument of this section. Present grief and pain may prove to be more beneficial in their effect on us than all the festivity, mirth, and jovial laughter of the outwardly prosperous man. Solomon makes his point with various proverbs and with Hebrew words of similar sound (a figure of speech called paronomasia) in verse 1 ("name," in Hebrew pronounced *shem*, and "perfume," Hebrew *shemen* and verses 5 and 6 ("Song," Hebrew *shir;* "pot," Hebrew *sir;* "thorns," Hebrew *sirim,* or, as we would attempt to reproduce this assonance in part in English, "As the noise of *nettles* under the *kettle*").

In verse 1, Solomon points to those things that are more abiding than the rich man's mirth. A good reputation (name) has an influence (the aroma of the perfume) beyond its owner. The day of a man's death also has a lasting influence, for afterward his life can be held forth as an example if his name has merited it.

The second proverb, in verse 2, is not much different from what our Lord said in the Sermon on the Mount: "Blessed are they that mourn" (Matthew 5:4). There is a mellowing that takes place in affliction and sorrow. To be in the presence of sickness or death has a tendency to bring us quickly to the really crucial issues of life. Likewise the third proverb, in verses 3-4, teaches that there is a lesson to be gained from and a work to be accomplished by sorrow.

Contrariwise, the prattle and laughter of fools (vv. 5-6) is useless, hollow, and bothersome. We, with David, should much more prefer the kind smiting and rebuke of the righteous (Psalm 141:5).

When the head of a ruler or judge is turned by

rewards in exchange for his oppression of someone's enemy, we can be sure that such a bribe will "destroy the heart;" that is, corrupt his understanding and blind his sense of justice and values (7:7).

In all cases, it is better to wait for God's timing than to be impatient (7:8-9). To worry unnecessarily or prematurely is to give way to a fool's approach to problems. Neither must we wish for the good old days, with their real or imaginary advantages and pleasures in comparison to the present situation (7:10). Surely, true wisdom would view things differently (7:11-12). Of such wisdom Solomon wrote in Proverbs: "Whoever finds me, finds life" (Proverbs 8:35); and "The fear of the Lord, this is wisdom" (Proverbs 1:7; 9:10; see also Job 28:28).

The truth of the matter is that affliction is the appointment of God (7:13-14). The "crooked" needing straightening (v. 13; cf. 1:15) is the presence of afflictions and adversities in life. No wonder the text exclaims (to paraphrase the point):

> Look with wonder, admire, and silently wait for the result of God's work! The contrasts of life are deliberately allowed by God so that men should ultimately develop a simple trust and dependence in God.
>
> For prosperity and the goods from God's hand, be thankful and rejoice. But in adversity and the crookedness of life, think. Reflect on the goodness of God and the comprehensiveness of His plan for men.

Therefore, although men appear to be treated irrespective of their character in the providence of God (7:15), the just man perishing in his righteousness and

Quality Living

the evil man apparently prolonging his life in his wickedness, this is again only "judging a book by its cover." Such a verdict is premature and improperly based. We must penetrate more deeply beneath the surface if we are to properly evaluate either of these men or the plan and ordinance of God.

Questions for Discussion

1. What is the conclusion of Ecclesiastes 6:1—8:15?
2. Read 6:1—7:15. Identify the complementary arguments that help us gain a proper view of the plan of God.
3. Discuss the irony of Ecclesiastes 6:2. What is the point of this verse?
4. How may we best sum up the truth set forth in 7:1-15?
5. Examine the list of proverbs in Ecclesiastes 7. What is Solomon's point in using them?
6. How do the main points and conclusions of Ecclesiastes 6:1—7:15 and 7:16-29 relate to 8:1-15?

9

Evaluating Man's Character

Solomon has warned us that if we are to properly reconcile the ways of God with the disappointments of men, we must avoid judging by mere externals. A second consideration is now introduced: those whom we suppose to be experiencing unfair suffering may not be as good as we suppose them to be.

Few verses in Ecclesiastes are more susceptible to incorrect interpretations than 7:16-18. For many, Solomon's advice is the so-called golden mean; it is as if he had said: "Don't be too holy and don't be too wicked. Sin to a moderate degree!" What such commentators miss is that verses 16-17 are not cautioning against possessing too much real righteousness. The danger is that men might delude themselves and others through a multiplicity of pseudoreligious acts of sanctimoniousness; ostentatious showmanship in the art of worship; a spirit of hypercriticism against minor deviations from one's own cultural norms, which are equated with God's righteousness; and a disgusting conceit and supercilious, holier-than-thou attitude veneered over the whole mess.

The real clue to this passage, as George R. Castellino demonstrated, is that the second verb in verse 16 "to be wise," must be rendered reflexively (Hebrew

Hithpael form), as "to think oneself to be furnished with wisdom." Furthermore, Castellino observed, even if this valid point about the reflexive nature of the verb is rejected for some reason, "Do not be wise" in verse 16 is to be understood as it is in Proverbs 3:7: "Be not wise *in your own eyes.*"[1] Accordingly, verse 17 would follow the same pattern as established for verse 16, because the two verses are part of the same thought. The resulting translation for verses 16-17 is:

> 7:16: Do not multiply [your] righteousness and do not play the part of the wise [in your own eyes; see Proverbs 3:7]—why destroy yourself?
>
> 7:17: Do not multiply [your] wickedness and do not be a [downright] fool—why die before your time?

The correctness of this interpretation can be demonstrated by its compatibility with verse 18. It is good, says Solomon, that men should take hold of "this," namely, true wisdom that comes from the fear of God, rather than grasping "that," namely, the folly of fools. It is the fear of God, that is the best protection against either absurdity. Neither man's folly nor a conceited and strained righteousness will serve as a guide or as a guise to mask the real need of men. They must come

---

1. George R. Castellino, "Qoheleth and His Wisdom," *Catholic Biblical Quarterly* 30 (1968): 24. See also R. N. Whybray, "Qoheleth the Immoralist? (Qoh. 7:16-17)," in *Israelite Wisdom: Theological and Literary Essays in Honor of Samuel Terrien*, ed. John G. Gammie (Missoula, Mont.: Scholars, 1978), pp. 191-204.

Evaluating Man's Character

to fear Him. That is true wisdom. Wisdom is then not a self-imposed estimate of one's own abilities. Indeed, true wisdom will be a better protection against all these errors and excesses than ten rulers or sultans in a city (v. 19).

We cannot be too careful in our evaluation of the character of men. Too much passes for true piety that is not piety at all. The only thing a pseudopious kind of scrupulosity will yield is the judgment of God. Therefore, warns Qoheleth, let us not be too quick to label the providence of God as unjust.

In fact, rather than being pious, no one is without fault in deed or word (vv. 20-22). Men are universally depraved, and we all fall short of the glory of God. The advantage (v. 20 begins with a "because") of the recommended wisdom in fearing God (v. 18) is that it does more than open up the pattern of meaning to the eternity of all things here below and above (3:11); this wisdom will also give men and women a self-control that will not resent the ill-advised slander, abuse, and curses of others. It is foolish to be overly concerned about and troubled by what others think and say about us in their unguarded, unkind, and foolish moments (vv. 21-22).

Nevertheless, it still must be said of even the wisest of us that despite the original uprightness of man as he came from the hand of His Maker in the Garden of Eden, we have one and all alike gone after our own scheme (v. 29). This truth could be set forth in a hyperbole: There is only one in a million (the Hebrew says a "thousand") who acts as he ought (v. 28). Sin has worked its corrosive effects on the entire human race. Therefore, those who discover wisdom—that is the subject of this section (vv. 20-29)—are very few indeed.

Why does Solomon appear to lock women out of those few who do find wisdom? "I did not find one woman among all of them," he complained in verse 28. He did not reflect any kind of chauvinism in Proverbs 12:4; 14:1; 18:22; and 19:14. In fact, wisdom for Solomon was personified as a woman. Had he suddenly overlooked the resourceful "judge Deborah," the devout Hannah, or the prophetic song leader Miriam of the past?

Solomon does not fit the usual definition of a misogynist—he? A woman hater? No, that wasn't *his* problem. Some commentators have suggested that this woman whose heart is a snare and a trap (v. 26) is but the personification of that wickedness which is folly itself. She is the "strange woman" of Proverbs 1-9. Perhaps this interpretation is the closest to what Solomon intended, for the topic is wisdom from 7:20 to 8:1. Therefore, never has that seductress been found, the very opposite of the woman wisdom herself, who knows the explanation of these things (8:1).

Character is not built by multiplied acts of ostentatious worship, nor is it to be presumed to be just naturally a part of all men and women. Unfortunately, just the reverse is true. Foolishness and sin are so much a part of humanity that only by submitting to the Lord in the fear of God will anyone be able to understand both the wisdom of God and the stupidity of wickedness. We are warned, then, that just as we must not "judge a book by its cover," so also we must not presume that the inner character of a man is

Evaluating Man's Character 111

always what we think it is on the basis of a limited knowledge of the alleged worship of men.

Questions for Discussion

1. Read Ecclesiastes 7:16-18. What do these verses teach?
2. What is true wisdom? What is the advantage of such wisdom?
3. Read Ecclesiastes 9:28. How is this verse to be understood?
4. Elaborate on the verb "to be wise" in verse 16. How does its interpretation concur with Proverbs 3:7?
5. What main truth do we learn from Ecclesiastes 7:16-29?

10

The Role of Human Government in God's Plan

Wisdom that comes from the fear of God can solve such enigmas (8:1) as those contemplated in the third section of this book. It can dispel the gloom and brighten man's otherwise hard looks.

A wise man realizes that chief among God's agents of justice presently available is the divine institution of human government (8:2-5). The doctrine presented here is exactly the same doctrine as that given by Paul in Romans 13:1-5. Human government is God's ordained means of rectifying most current disorders.

Foremost among Solomon's commands in this section is obedience to "the powers that be" (8:2). The reasons for this obedience to a human institution are:

- Subjects are obligated by an oath of allegiance, whether they are foreigners who are required to give an oath or native-born citizens who are also under a covenant to obey (8:2).
- The ruler has authority to enforce what he commands ("He does whatever he pleases" 8:3*b*-4*a*) when subjects get involved in an evil cause.
- There is safety and wisdom in keeping the king's

commandment; subjects need not "feel any evil thing" (8:5*a*).
- Wise men are able to discern in their hearts the appropriate time and procedure for doing the king's will (8:5*b*), for as 3:1 argued, there is an appropriate and divinely appointed time and procedure for every matter (8:6).

Those arguments are further elaborated in Romans 13:1-7, Titus 3:1, and 1 Peter 2:13-18.

The purpose of government is the righteous administration of justice. When rulers and judges carry out that divine mandate, both they and their people are blessed by God, and a considerable amount of man's present distress is alleviated.

Unfortunately, those in authority are not always faithful to their mandate. In verse 9, it has to be sadly conceded that rulers often inflict injustices on their subjects. This was duly noted by Solomon and provided for in the wise plan of God. Still, in spite of every perversion, God's purpose is accomplished.

The ultimate fulfillment of God's purpose is also the transition point in 8:5*b*. In language reminiscent of 3:1 we move from human government as God's means of correcting current disorders to God's supreme control over all. The only addition here over the teaching of 3:1 is that besides noting that the excellent plan of God has a set time for everything, Solomon also observes here that there is a judgment set aside for all the wicked (8:6, 13).

Ignorance of the plan and times of God increases man's misery; man is particularly miserable because he cannot avoid death (8:6-8). God has vested the control of all things in His own hands and not in the hands of mortals. And because he is ignorant of God's workings, man, not God, is responsible for all the misery endured on earth as he tries to do things contrary to God's will.

Even though men may be wrongly encouraged in their evil deeds by the abuse of power and position by those in authority (8:9), the wicked receiving honorable burials (8:10) and delays being allowed in the administration of justice (8:11), it will be well nevertheless for those who fear God (8:12-13). "Fear" appears three times in 8:12-13 to denote those who truly and habitually fear God. There will be a day, as Micah 3:18 also says, when you will be able to discern the difference between those who feared God and those who refused to fear Him. Then a most exacting justice shall be meted out. The wicked may appear to be getting away with murder ("one hundred times," v. 12), but such sinning with seeming impunity will finally be judged by the living God.

That the just deserts of the wicked often seem to fall on the righteous God-fearer while the rewards of the righteous appear to drop into the lap of the wicked is understandable only by the wisdom found in the fear of God, the plan of God, and the ability to enjoy life as offered by God to all who trust Him.

The mystery is now solved, so far as its main outlines are concerned. How refreshing, in contrast to the mad search of empty, plastic men who are shaped by their evil desires and the current trends in thought, is the contented capacity to enjoy the gifts given by a loving, all-wise God to those who have first sought the kingdom of God and His righteousness (8:15). God's gift of enjoyment is to be preferred over all accumulations that the wicked possess and for which they are tempted to act so wickedly in obtaining them apart from the plan of God.

Questions for Discussion

1. Read Ecclesiastes 8:2-5 (cf. Romans 13:1-7; Titus 3:1; 1 Peter 2:13-18). What reasons did Solomon give for obedience to a human institution?
2. What is the purpose of government? Can a human government fulfill this purpose?
3. What is to be our response when our government fails to live up to its God-ordained responsibility?
4. What is man's consequence of ignoring God's plan and times?
5. Discuss Solomon's conclusion in Ecclesiastes 8:15.

Part 4

Removing Discouragements and Applying God's Plan to the Lives of Believers

Ecclesiastes 8:16—12:14

The fourth and final section of Ecclesiastes does not open up additional arguments but merely supplements what has already been affirmed. Men and women must be given some practical advice and taught how to apply the insights gained from the new perspective on life provided in the first three sections. The righteous must be encouraged lest the enigmas that still remain in the mystery of God are allowed to dishearten them. Thus the argument of the third section is strengthened and supplemented with practical admonitions.

As in the previous three units of Ecclesiastes, so also in this fourth section there are three divisions and a conclusion.

1. 8:16—9:9: The remaining mystery in this subject must not diminish human joy.
2. 9:10—11:6: The remaining mystery in this subject must not prevent us from working with all our might.
3. 11:7—12:8: The daily reminder of our imminent death and the prospect of facing our Creator and Judge should infect all our God-given joy and activity.
Conclusion 12:9-14

Rather than begin with the conclusion as we have done in the previous three sections, the conclusion in this case also serving as the epilogue to the whole book of Ecclesiastes, this section will be treated in the order that it appears in the text, because the trend of Solomon's thought and argument is clear by now.

11

Applying God's Plan to the Joy of Life

How vast a scope does the writer's ambitious inquiry into the affairs of men cover—the total range of man's labor on earth. Yet in spite of all the acknowledged injustice, evil, and crooked deals in the world, man's work is identified with "all the work of God." Now there is a first-class "mystery" in the biblical sense of the word: something we know somewhat better because of God's disclosure on the subject, but which still contains baffling aspects. Even after we have been treated to an elaborate discussion of the plan of God as it affects the most mundane features of life, and even after we have been warned that the alleged inequalities in the divine plan are often mere hasty inferences made by anxious men, with somewhat shocking but refreshing candor Solomon asserts that there still are some insoluble mysteries in divine providence. No one can know entirely what goes on under the sun (8:17). Men can search and dig for such wisdom as much as they wish, but they will discover that they will be as shut out from their desired goal as the man who went on the same quest for wisdom in Job 28. The author of Job 28 plainly declared: "Man does not know the way to [wisdom]" (Job 28:13), for only "God understands the way" (Job 28:23). In fact, God said to man, "The fear of the Lord, that is wisdom; and to depart from evil is discernment" (Job 28:28). No wonder, then, that even so-called wise men cannot know what goes on under the sun. Human insight, understanding, and reason, like water, cannot rise higher than their source or own level. Therefore, to the degree that God reveals His plan to believers, to that degree only are they able to apprehend that much of the plan of God. Yet there still is mystery left. Only God knows entirely; we mortals know only in part.

Should the above concession lead to despair, let it be quickly stated that the righteous and the truly wise who fear the Lord are "in the hands of God" (9:1). The apostle Paul stated the same truth later: "The Lord knows those that are His" (2 Timothy 2:19). Our quest for identity, meaning, and an explanation of the presence of evil, injustice, and inequities in life must end where Solomon's did—in the fact that God sits at the helm, ruling and overruling for good. Consequently, His people, their works, and their very lives are protected and governed by the God who is over all. They are safe in His hands.

JOY IN THE FACE OF SUFFERING (9:1-6)

In spite of all that has been said to explain and justify the ways of God to man, there are some mysteries in divine providence. No one can tell just by God's treatment of particular individuals whether they are objects of God's love or hatred (9:1). Qoheleth warned in 6:1-6 that prosperity is not always or necessarily a good thing and in 7:1-15 that adversity and affliction are not always or necessarily evil. God's approval or disapproval of us cannot always be read from "all that is before [us]" (9:1); things are not always what they seem to be to us or what our friends construe them to be. After all, Job's three friends took the bare facts of his suffering and incorrectly concluded that he must have sinned grievously; otherwise he would not have been suffering as he was. Nor must we conclude that God hates those to whom He sends adversity and loves those who receive prosperity. If believers are to walk by faith, there will be times when outward appearances and facts will defy explanation for the moment. It is cruel to add to the hurt of oppressed persons by suggesting that they are definitely objects of God's judgment. Such narrow-minded reasoning would suggest that all suffering is the result of personal sin, but that would be unbiblical. Certainly some suffering is (1) *doxological*, for the glory of God (as Jesus showed His disciples for proper deduction to be drawn from the man born blind in John 9:1-3); some is (3) *probationary* as when Habakkuk looked out from his watchtower on a world of tyranny, violence, and sin and found the answer in patient waiting for God's long-suffering retribution to take effect); some is (4) *revelational* (as the prophet Hosea learned the isolation felt by God as a result of Israel's spiritual adultery when he, Hosea, lost his own wife in physical harlotries); and some suffering is (5) *sacrificial* (as the suffering Servant bore great pain because of the sin of others [Isaiah 42; 49-50; 53]). Therefore it is most unfortunate when men hastily make a one-to-one nexus between personal guilt and suffering.

If one argues that this association between suffering and personal guilt is frequently witnessed when the Bible addresses nations and institutions such as bodies of believers, we agree. But nations and local churches have no continuing existence in the life to come; therefore, their judgment must be rendered in God's justice here and now. Individuals, however, will personally stand before God in that day to come.

But to return to the text of Ecclesiastes, the mystery before us in 9:2-6 is the most perplexing of all life's puzzles: the presence of sin and death in God's good world ruled by God's good plan.

Now Solomon does not level a charge against God when he labels what happens to good and evil men alike as an "evil" (9:3). His use of this term "evil," like his evaluation, is strictly from the human point of view and based on appearances. He has, for the moment, purposely left out all considerations of the divine perspective and revelational facts. Thus, so far as men can see, one "event," or "destiny," comes to all.

The word translated "fate," or "fortune" (9:2, 3), in some versions of the Bible should instead be translated "event": "one event comes to all." Solomon refers only to that which "meets" men at the end of their lives, an "event," a "happening," or "outcome" (Hebrew *miqreh*). There is not one hint in this term of anything of the power of fate as found in paganism.

The momentary absence of all distinction between the righteous and the wicked in that all must die is a mystery above all mysteries. Why should profane swearers and irreligious and godless men who abstain from sacrificing and practicing good (9:2) be accorded the same treatment as those who deserve better? It is difficult to understand: the wicked share that "one event" with the good. The wicked, whose hearts are full of evil and every conceivable madness while they are alive, join their righteous counterparts and go to the grave.

Verse 4 makes the point necessary for practical men: Where there is life, there is hope. The actual translation of the verse is not as easy as is the sense. The Hebrew and many ancient versions say, "What then is to be chosen? With all the living there is hope." There was, however, a Hebrew tradition of reading (called the *Qere*) this text that supposed that two letters ought to be transposed in the verb "to choose" (*y^ebuchar*) to make it "to join" (*yechubbar*), and thus the verse would read, "For whosoever is joined to all the living, he has hope." Both translations are possible, and the sense is not measurably different in either case. (Most commentators and versions have a slight preference for the latter reading.) Solomon's point is plain: While men are still alive there is hope—hope of preparation for meeting God, hope of living significantly, hope of doing something to the glory of God before all men personally face Him as 12:14 warns, when man will give a detailed accounting of his life to determine if it has been lived in a manner well-pleasing to God.

The proverb is verse 4*b*, a proverb also found in Arabic, reinforces the significance of life. As lowly and despicable a creature as a dog is (from the viewpoint of the ancient Near Eastern mentality), it is still far preferable to be a live dog than to be a mighty, majestic, exalted—but dead—lion. Life! That is the precious item!

Gloom seems to settle ever so densely when verses 5-6 are reached. Are these verses a flat denial of any hope for a life beyond the grave? Is it the settled opinion of Qoheleth that when one is dead, he becomes extinct—knowing nothing and finished with everything, including loving, hating, envying, and inheriting?

On the contrary, the reference to all those things is strictly limited to things as they are enjoyed "under the sun" and on this side of immortality. Qoheleth does not deny that men may receive an inheritance in the hereafter. His point, the same as in John's gospel, is exceedingly important: "Work while it is still day, for the night comes when no man can work" (John 9:4*b*). It is the consciousness that men will soon die and no longer be able to relate to the needs and joys of this life that forces the striking contrast of verses 5-6. Knowledge in this life, rewards for this life, and opportunities for service are serious challenges when viewed from the prospect of our soon-to-appear death. If men are going to live as if there is no tomorrow in eternity and let their passions and desires have free reign, they will have played the real fool's role. Thus, although death is still an enigma, men must not pretend to live as if they "only go around once in this world" (to borrow the sorry philosophy of some current Madison Avenue advertising). How sad it would be to have lost all opportunity to share in doing anything significant to the glory of God.

JOY, THE GIFT OF GOD AND GRACE OF LIFE (9:7-9)

What, then, should be done? The righteous know. They must rejoice and enjoy life, for "this is the day that the Lord has made; [they] will be glad and rejoice in it" (Psalm 118:24). Instead of allowing grief to consume one's life, Solomon urges that whatever remains of the unexplained mystery in our lives must not prevent us from enjoying life. The tendency to brood and to mope about has to be resisted in the lives of those who fear God, take life as a gift from His hand, and receive God's plan and enablement to enjoy that life. Accordingly, verse 7 begins with an invitation: "Come on"; be up and about. Eat your food, drink your wine, get out your white set of clothes, shampoo your head with the most luxurious of oils, and enjoy the domestic comfort and love of your wife (9:7-9), "For God has long since accepted your works" (9:7). Righteous men need not worry whether God is indifferent to them and their lives: He is not; they are the special objects of His gifts and His acceptance.

Wine and bread, the staff of life, are frequently representative in Scripture of that which God gives to comfort and cheer us (Genesis 14:18; 1 Samuel 16:20; 25:18; Nehemiah 5:15; Ecclesiastes 10:19; Lamentations 2:12). Likewise, white garments and ointments were symbols of joy and purity, as John illustrated in his word to the church of Sardis in Revelation 3:4-5:

> You have a few persons, even in Sardis,
> who have not defiled their garments;
> they shall walk with me in white: for they are worthy.
> He that overcomes, the same shall be clothed
>   in white clothing (cf. Revelation 19:8).

Because ordinary people could not maintain and perpetually clean their cool and pleasant white garments as could people of wealth and rank, they reserve such clothes for especially important or festive occasions.

Accordingly, white garments became emblems of joy and festivity. The same was true of perfuming, or anointing, oneself with oils.

Neither is the joy of marriage to be left out of life. Celibacy, or abstinence, is not a holier state than matrimony, for the point Qoheleth is making is the same as that of the writer of the book of Hebrews: marriage is honorable and the marriage bed is undefiled (Hebrews 13:4). So, to the festive delights of verses 7-8, Solomon adds the gratifications, comforts and delights of enjoying life with your wife whom you love (9:9). Literally the Hebrew text reads: "See life with your wife you love." This expression "to see" was used in a more comprehensive manner than we use it today in the West. Ginsburg said that the verb "to see" was used of those who were in the midst of experiencing any of the full range of human emotions and passions (e.g., see Ecclesiastes 2:1).[1] Thus Solomon's advice is to go ahead, get married, and enjoy the delights of married love and companionship instead of worrying about the remaining mystery in the plan of God. Do not even try to fully comprehend why you enjoy the gifts mentioned in verses 7-9. Receive them for what they are, gifts, and receive God's ability to partake of them with pleasure. Would not Peter add later that beautiful phrase, "Live considerately with your wives . . . since you are joint heirs of the grace of life" (1 Peter 3:7)?

The tone of this injunction sets the context for un-

---

1. Christian D. Ginsburg, *Coheleth, Commonly Called the Book of Ecclesiastes* [1861; reprinted in *The Song of Songs and Coheleth (Commonly Called the Book of Ecclesiastes)*, The Library of Biblical Studies, ed. Harry M. Orlinsky, New York: Ktav, 1970], p. 425.

derstanding Solomon's earlier word on women in 7:26-28. He was definitely not a misogynist. He was fully aware of what a beautiful gift a true wife is. Men should abstain from marriage only if they are given the gift of celibacy (1 Corinthians 7:7) or if the times are so perilous that marriage would be an added pressure and not a joy (Jeremiah 16:1-4; 1 Corinthians 7:26, 29).

Be joyful, then, and receive God's gifts and His ability to enjoy them. Why should anyone who truly fears God have the joy of life stolen out from under him because of the unresolved perplexities still remaining in the partially disclosed plan of God? Rejoice and be exceedingly glad, for these are the gifts that the Lord has made; we should rejoice and be glad in them (to paraphrase the words of Psalm 118:24). To be sure, the "joy of the Lord is [our] strength" (Nehemiah 8:10), and in that stronghold and tower the righteous take refuge during life's journey.

Qoheleth urges acceptance of the grace and joy of life, not pessimism, nihilism, and blind determinism. Believers are to be rebuked for rejecting God's worldly gifts and refusing to use them in a proper way. Out of a distorted view of worldliness, wherein every pleasure ordained by God for man's enjoyment is either denied or begrudgingly used, many have developed a superpious, unhappy, and even miserable existence. This text proclaims liberation to them. Brother and sister: rejoice in God's good gifts, and ask for His ability rightfully to use them.

Questions for Discussion
1. Read Ecclesiastes 8:16—9:9. What is the theme of this passage?

2. Name the five kinds of suffering described by Dr. Kaiser.
3. Read Ecclesiastes 9:2-6. How do we resolve this puzzle? How did Solomon resolve it?
4. What is the significance of the proverb in Ecclesiastes 9:4*b*? What did Solomon intend to teach by it?
5. Discuss the emphasis in Ecclesiastes 9:5-6 on the finality of death. What was Solomon's point? How may we apply the truth of those verses to our lives?
6. Read Dr. Kaiser's literal translation of Ecclesiastes 9:9. What should be our response to it?

12

Applying God's Plan to Our Work

It must be conceded that men do not always obtain the results they expect (9:11-12), but not even that should stop believers from working with the utmost energy (9:10).

WORK WHILE IT IS YET DAY (9:10-12)

The time to labor for God is while we are still on this side of the grave, for when death comes, the day of opportunity will have passed. The phrasing of verse 10 is reminiscent of Colossians 3:23: "Whatever your task, do it heartily, as unto the Lord and not to men." Men must not opt out of total, earnest, and dedicated involvement in the privilege of work. They may think that the presence of evil and their impending death are massive obstacles to believing that God has a good plan for all of life, and therefore they may refuse to do anything pending further disclosures on the subject. But such inactivity is wrong. Counsels the teacher, "Get involved and work vigorously" to the glory of God while you still have life in your bones.

Once again, Solomon warns, "There is no work, no

planning, no knowledge, and no wisdom in the grave [*Sheol*] where you are going" (9:10). But as in 9:5-6, so here: this affirmation is no denial of a future state or of personal, conscious presence with God immediately after death of the body. The point is that in relation *to this world* (9:6), those possibilities have ceased. To make the words of 9:10 into an absolute denial of immorality would be as unfair as doing the same to Jesus' words in John 9:4: "The night comes when no man can work."

The Hebrew word *Sheol* occurs about sixty-five times in the Old Testament and is already correctly translated as "grave" in approximately half of those instances. In my judgment, all sixty-five could be equally well rendered "grave." This does not deny the existence of the doctrine of a place for the departed, unbelieving dead, namely, hell; it only raises the question whether this particular word should be translated that way in all or any of its contexts. Certainly in this verse the rendering "grave" fills the bill well.

Therefore, while the resources of life are still at hand—ability to *do* work, faculties to *devise*, or brainstorm, new ideas, and ability to use the almost daily accumulation of knowledge and *wisely* apply it to the situations of life (9:10)—put your whole self and strength into each task.

To further stimulate men to action, Solomon makes three supporting arguments that may be stated in the following proverb (9:11-12):

- It is not in man that walks to direct his steps (Jeremiah 10:23).

Applying God's Plan to Our Work 131

- The Lord may save by many or by few (1 Samuel 14:6).
- Time and events [destiny] come to all (Ecclesiastes 9:11).

Advantages and resources often mean very little if God is not in those talents. In quick order Solomon ticks off five assets enjoyed by men who would appear to be the most likely to succeed: the "swift," the "strong," the "wise," the "discerning," and the "learned." Who was swifter than Asahel, who fell needlessly, smitten by the butt end of Abner's spear (2 Samuel 2:22-23)? Who was stronger than Samson, but who was weaker before women (Judges 16:19)? Who was wiser than Solomon, but who was more indulgent in sin? (1 Kings 11:1-25)? Who was more discerning than Ahithophel, but who was so easily supplanted by Hushai and his foolish counsel (2 Samuel 16:23; 17:5-14)? Who was more learned in all the ways of the Egyptians than Moses, yet who also preempted every agency of justice in rushing into murder (Exodus 2:11-15; Acts 7:22)?

In the divine plan of things, the race belongs to the one who runs in the strength of God. Strength, wisdom, speed, discernment, and learning are only valuable in-so-far as they are offered by God. "Time and events happen to them all" (9:11), observed Qoheleth. The second subject of the sentence, "events," is not to be rendered "chance." The word (Hebrew *pega^{c}c*) simply means an "occurrence," and comes from the verb "to meet" (cf. 1 Kings 5:4). It is true, however, that the "occurrence," or "event," is usually an *evil* occurrence. Because the verb shared by this compound subject is singular (*yiqreh*, "to come, happen"), the idea is a compact one. The "time" is a time of judgment to be directed by God, in whom He may allow the events and situations of life to overwhelm and overthrow those whose endowment of abilities seems to deny the possibility of their ever failing. It is a vain thing to trust in any human qualities rather than in the living God. The same truth is taught in Proverbs 21:30, "There is no wisdom, no discernment, and no counsel that can prevail against the Lord;" and in 1 Samuel 17:47, "The Lord does not deliver with the sword or the spear, for the battle belongs to the Lord" (see also 2 Chronicles 20:15).

Human ability cannot guarantee success. In fact, more frequently than not, those who trust the most in their own abilities are the very persons who are caught unsuspectingly and suddenly by their own devices. Those who appear to be doing so well in this life end up being the greatest losers around. "If we could see beyond today as God can see," sang the songwriter. But we would conclude his song somewhat differently to fit the truth here: "Then we would not begin to doubt and often complain." When men do not pay attention to the fact that their "time" of judgment is ever near, they are trapped, just as fish and birds are caught in nets (v. 12). Believers must not judge these books by the covers; things are not what they appear to be. God is in charge. Men will be judged. Men must diligently work with all their might to the glory of God in every aspect of life, for the night is coming when the opportunity will be lost and all of life will be reviewed by the God who knows absolutely what is right and what is wrong.

GOD-GIVEN WISDOM IS OF THE UTMOST IMPORTANCE IN OUR WORK (9:13-18)

As an illustration of the great advantage to be found in the employment of wise action, a parable is cited in 9:13-16. The situation is one of remarkable contrast: a small city with few men in it was besieged by a great king with the latest in armaments and military might. But the apparently unstoppable king was outmaneuvered. There was in that same besieged city a poor but wise man who delivered the small city from the great king. The shame of the matter was that no one remembered who the wise man was; neither was he ever properly honored or rewarded. Thus, although that poor, wise man failed to profit personally from his labors, his wisdom was not profitless for others or for this world.

The conclusions to be drawn from this parable are found in 9:16-18. (1) Wisdom, that gift that comes from the fear of God (Proverbs 1:7, 29; 2:56; 8:13; 15:33), is a greater asset than strength, even though it is despised and left unheeded by the masses (9:16*a*). Such a triumph of wisdom over brute force as in the parable of 9:13-16 was no doubt fresh in Solomon's mind. For when David's general, Joab, besieged the small city of Abel in Israel, where the insurrectionist Sheba had taken refuge, a wise woman called to Joab from the city wall and delivered the city in her wisdom (2 Samuel 20:16-22).

134   Quality Living

The other side of the coin is that (2) wisdom is not always heeded (9:16*b*). Only in emergencies can the quiet words of wisdom be heard. Therefore, (3) men must have a certain mental disposition and spirit of receptivity if wisdom is to be heard (9:17). The clamor of demagogues and self-styled bosses is a striking contrast of works of quiet instruction delivered by wise men of God. (4) "Wisdom is power," to restate an old proverb, but one sinner (or ruler) who in his folly and self-willed obstinacy refuses to accept "wisdom" thereby destroys much good and many a kingdom, too (9:18).

RESULTS OF FOOLISH AND WISE WORKS ARE CONTRASTED (10:1-20)

To reinforce his admonition about the value of wisdom, Solomon in chapter 10 exhibits the same thought in a series of loosely connected maxims in the style of the book of Proverbs. Just as we argued that 3:2-8 does not refer to various stages in a Christian's growth process or even to seven periods of the church, so chapter 10 is not a chapter of connected teachings on rulers (verses 4-7, 16-17, 20) or the evils of ill-conceived attempts to overthrow bad governments (verses 8-10, 18-19).

Therefore, what 10:1 does is to illustrate the last statement in 9:18 from an everyday incident. Just as one "dead fly" (or, more accurately, "flies that bring death," i.e., by their excrement) affects the entire batch of costly ointment, so a little folly can display itself as mightier and more glorious than the genuine wisdom of a poor, wise man who could deliver his small city from the hands of a great king. There is a related Arabic proverb: "A fly is nothing, yet it produces loathsomeness." So a little bit of foolishness, although as insignificant as a fly (we would say a flea), is nonetheless able to muster great power in the eyes of men. Solomon does not refer to that trace of folly in a wise man or the lapses of the otherwise good man; he instead refers to the tendency for folly to predominate over "honorable wisdom" (note in the Hebrew for 10:1*b* the word *Min,* meaning "than," or "a comparison").

But appearances must not deceive believers, for the "heart" (i.e., the mind, or inner nature) of a wise man is ever ready to protect him from numerous dangers (10:2)—on his right hand. The right hand is not a reference to good luck and the left to ill fortune, for the Bible has no belief in a goddess of fortune. As Ginsburg noted, to be on one's right was to defend or be ready to assist one,[1] as in Psalm 16:8; 121:5. To keep men from concluding that wisdom was *absolutely* useless, Solomon again qualified that implication by showing wisdom's relative advantages and merits. The fool, meanwhile, "misses his mind," or is absent from it. His heart and mind are useless to him in emergencies.

The fool exposes himself as soon as he sets foot outside his door (10:3). Whether "on the way" is meant literally or figuratively (for his life-style and

---

1. Christian D. Ginsburg, *Coheleth, Commonly Called the Book of Ecclesiastes* [1861; reprinted in *The Song of Songs and Coheleth (Commonly Called the Book of Ecclesiastes),* The Library of Biblical Studies, ed. Harry M. Orlinsky, New York: Ktav, 1970], p. 425.

dealings with men) makes little difference. In all of life, he openly proclaims that he is a fool to all who meet him. Wisdom is much more to be preferred than all of this in verses 1-3.

But another issue arises in 10:4-7; namely, the wisdom of patiently submitting to the anger of tyrannical rulers because, as 8:16-17 stated at the beginning of this section, men are not always able to tell just why certain things are done. The wisdom embodied in verse 4 was later expressed, as Genung observed,[2] in the beatitude, "Blessed are the meek" (Matthew 5:5). Solomon had taught the same truth in Proverbs 16:14, and the subject of his remarks, no doubt, was not his own royal practices, but the practices of those who ruled in the countries around Israel.

In this connection of pacifying anger aroused by great errors, "There is an evil," says Qoheleth in one of his favorite introductory phrases (10:5; cf. 5:13; 6:9). Yet in line with the wise and meek attitude he has just counseled in the preceding verse (v. 4), he continues, "Such an error" gives evidence that not everything rulers do is always perfect and fair. This blot on the record of human governments is another one of those enigmas in the divine plan: Why does God allow such foolishness to continue?

The blunder and error of human governments can often be seen in this tragedy: rulers put their foolish favorites into office over those who are more qualified (10:5-6). Such strangers to the fear of God are called fools. Meanwhile, those who by birth and train-

---

2. John F. Genung, *Words of Koheleth* (New York: Houghton, Mifflin, 1904), p. 331.

ing are more qualified for such government posts are passed by. These errors are the natural fruit of partiality, tyranny, and despotism. If the ruler had used wisdom, he would have chosen the "nobles" (literally "the rich"), whose ability to accumulate and handle wealth might have indicated the gifts of prudence and wisdom.

The arbitrariness of despotism is indicated by the frequent reversal of positions among the citizenry. In a culture in which only dignitaries were allowed the privilege of riding, there was a great social upheaval, as suggested by the complete reversal of normal roles—servants were riding horses while princes walked like menials at their side (10:7). Many have longed to know why such things are allowed by God to happen. If only—. But that is one part of God's plan that He has not been pleased to reveal to us in detail. The reality of such arbitrariness is freely granted by the text, but the text also warns us against permitting it to become a roadblock to joyful and active involvement in life.

No less disturbing are the series of difficulties posed in 10:8-11. The connection of thought between these verses and what preceded can be explained in any number of ways: (1) as Solomon's warnings against participating in the overthrow of despotic governments; (2) as a discussion of the difficulty of governing the masses; (3) as a reminder that Life is determined by what some call fate and not the wisdom of men; and (4) as a description of the unenviable end of those young upstarts who try to buck the system. Actually, the theme is still the contrasting results of the application of wisdom or folly to life's difficult situations. Wise, wholehearted activity will be tempered by meekness, or "patience" (Hebrew *marpe*). But in verses 8-11, the keyword is the "success" (Hebrew *haksher*) that wise action brings (v. 10*b*).

The warning of the five sentences preceding the concluding observation of 10:10*b* is that every course of action in life has its risk. If one is to succeed and emerge with "benefit," or "profit" (cf. the theme question of 1:3: "What's the *benefit* of all man's labor?"), he must act, but act wisely. That is the "margin" that counts. There is the "surplus" (*yitron*). The balance of power, observes Genung, is wisdom.[3] Wise men, unlike fools, take into their calculations the possible danger, and then they guard against it. The situations and their dangers are ordinary enough:

1. Digging pits	1. Falling into the pits
2. Breaking down walls	2. Being bitten by a serpent
3. Quarry stones	3. Being hurt by the stones
4. Splitting logs	4. Endangering oneself
5. Chopping wood	5. Overexertion because of dull axe

Wisdom is the difference between success and failure. It allows for something "left over," a "surplusage," and an "advantage" that contributes to the success of the task and the character of the worker. And wisdom must not be an afterthought added to one's work as perfume is added to complete the dressed-up person. Ecclesiastes 10:11 bemoans the uselessness of help that comes too late, like a charmer (or, as we

---

3. Ibid., p. 333.

would say, the snake catcher) who comes after the viper has already bitten someone. To use another proverb, Why lock the barn door after the cow has gotten out? The proper and wise use of the charmer's tongue could have prevented the disaster and been of "benefit" (*yitron*) to the afflicted.

Appropriately enough, there now follows a series of proverbs on using the tongue wisely while fools prattle away emptily (10:12-15). Wisdom is still the only proper guide to joyful involvement in life, despite life's pitfalls and inexplicable twists. Wisdom will temper, guard, and guide our actions—that is, true wisdom found in the fear of God. And the instrument of this wisdom will be the tongue, or words, of a wise man. His words are gracious in content, winsome in spirit, affectionate in appeal, and compliant and affable in tone.

On the other hand, the words of a fool work his own defeat and destruction—they "swallow him up" (10:12*b*). He is his own worst enemy. His words may be portrayed in a sort of gradation, where at first he is guilty of no more than mere silliness or nonsense;[4] but as he goes on from one folly to the next, he ends up in all sorts of extremism. There is nothing by which he can measure or guide his speech—it becomes sheer madness (10:13). He simply talks too much (10:14*a*), a constant stream of foolishness.

The pity is that the fool has no idea what he is talking about. He has no idea what the future holds. His unbelief and failure to consider that there is a future judgment, wherein the totality of life will be

---

4. Ibid., p. 334.

reviewed, puts him at such a huge disadvantage compared to the devout, wise man that he is to be pitied.

The rhetorical question about the fool's lack of knowledge of the future, or his deficiency in the area of some teacher who should tell him about the future (10:14b), is a valid reminder of a repeated Solomonic theme. The same question had been asked in 3:22, 6:12, 8:7, and in part in 9:12 to prepare the true seeker after God for the grand conclusion of 12:14: God—He alone—will bring every deed into judgment, whether good or evil. Foolish babblers are a dime a dozen, but revelation that is "in the know" is difficult to come by unless a wise man (12:9-11) teaches words of truth about man's future.

A fool will exert himself until he is blue in the face (and in vocabulary), but he will have little more effect than to tire men (10:15a). People will get sick of a self-styled religious demagogue's proclaiming God's death and the futility of any hope beyond the grave. The fool's lack of knowledge and discretion on such topics will be plain from his lack of good horse sense in any other area. If he doesn't know how to get from his place to town (10:15b), how can he be trusted when he pontificates on such topics as the hereafter? He is all talk. Genung described the fool's prattle in the words of Shakespeare's Macbeth as

> a tale told by an idiot, full of sound and fury, signifying nothing.[5]

Once more Qoheleth will enlist the services of wisdom in a fresh effort to aid men in the happy im-

---

5. Ibid., p. 336.

provement of their lives (10:16-20). With adroitness and the utmost care, Solomon warns that his previous discussion about the wisdom of obeying kings should not be taken as a blank check of approval for everything princes and rulers do. In verse 16, instead of directly attacking the ruler and princes, he denounces the "land" whose king is so foolish as to be childish and whose princes are so bold as to begin their drinking parties in the morning. Nevertheless, his meaning is clear: "Woe" to *them*.

But how fortunate is that land in which the king and his staff rule with wisdom (10:17).

Continuing the sad state of affairs in verse 16, verse 18 decries those rulers who indulge in luxury and intemperance, allowing the country to deteriorate and permitting abuses to flourish. Such a dilapidated and reckless maintenance of justice must be compared to the leaking of a house's roof, causing the roof to rot and, ultimately, collapse. This evil can be laid at the feet of one form of foolishness—downright laziness.

The land's misfortune through such foolishness is further compounded in 10:19 by the people's idleness and indulgence in laughter, feasts, and drinking, and money is their solution to everything: "Money answers every demand and every wish."

But as if to quickly caution the wise person not to be tempted to unwisely make a frontal attack on government just because some or most of the leaders lack credibility, Solomon adds verse 20. Be careful of disloyal speech that comes from disloyal thoughts. Influential members of the body politic may learn of your thoughts when some unseen events exposes you. The proverbial reference to the bird in verse 20 is like our proverb "The walls have ears" or "Some little bird told me." Thus Solomon advises discretion, caution, and control.

ACTIVE INVOLVEMENT IS PROPER, EVEN WHEN SUCCESS IS NOT GUARANTEED IN EVERY CASE (11:1-6)

Since we cannot comprehend the totality of God's providential acts, the only proper course of action is to be diligent and wholeheartedly involved; some of this activity will succeed even if all of it does not.

Serving as illustrations of this general advice, Solomon lists a half dozen everyday incidents to describe what he means. In 11:1 he advises that men "cast their bread on the waters," even when there is no assurance that they will benefit from that action. Indeed, they may "find it after many days," but nothing is guaranteed.

Delitzsch quotes a similar Aramaic proverb of Ben Sira: "Scatter thy bread on the water and on the dry land; in the end of the days thou findest it again." And there is a similar Arabic proverb: "Do good, cast thy bread into the water, thou shalt be repaid some day."[6]

As Ginsburg observed, Solomon, having just given us proverbs for dealing wisely with those *above* us, now gives us a proverb for dealing with those *below* us.[7] Thus, he is encouraging hospitality and patient trust in the ultimate rewards of God according to His master plan. The "bread on the water" may not be a literal reference to throwing thin cakes of bread into

---

6. Franz Delitzsch, *Commentary on the Song of Songs and Ecclesiastes*, trans. M. G. Easton (1877; reprinted in *Biblical Commentary on the Old Testament*, by C. F. Keil and Franz Delitzsch, Grand Rapids: Eerdmans, 1950), p. 391.
7. Ginsburg, p. 447.

the water like chips of wood in the hope that those cakes will one day turn up in some distant place where we will be—and there be in need of bread cakes! The figure may come instead from the realm of foreign commerce, wherein ships finally return with a gain after an indefinite period of time. Likewise, men and women must judiciously and courageously venture forth in benevolent charity without selfish motives, for such help must be given with the confidence that there is a dependable order and plan in the world and a "God who does all."

As if to make plain his meaning in verse 1, Qoheleth repeats his thought and develops it in verse 2. What had been said in the figure of "cast thy bread on the waters" is now said plainly and literally: "Give a portion to seven, even to eight." Of course the numbers here are not to limit such generosity to only eight individuals, nor are they an indication of uncertainty—seven or eight. Rather, this is the scriptural pattern of "X1," as, for example in Amos 1 and 2: "For three transgressions, yea four." "Be liberal and generous to as *many* as you can and *then some*," is the way we would say it. So, make as many friends as you can, for you never know when you yourself may need assistance. Instead of becoming miserly just because you fear that the future may hold some evil reversal of your fortunes, leaving you in poverty and want, you should all the more distribute to as many as possible so that you can have the blessing of receiving in the event of such reverses. In fact, says Proverbs 19:17, "The one who had pity on the poor lends to the Lord; and that which he gives will be paid back again" (see also Luke 16:9).

A third illustration is found in 11:3, which also

urges us to continued activity even though we are ignorant of the circumstances connected with our exertions. Full clouds will empty themselves on the earth even though some of the water seems to be wasted, falling on lakes, oceans, and uninhabited deserts. But some of the rain will be directly beneficial. Likewise, trees blown over in storms will fall on one man's property or another's. But someone will get the use of the firewood, so rejoice.

Similarly, man cannot tell what will come from any event in life. Yet the believer knows that whether he receives the evil of a flood, hurricane, tornado, or famine, or the blessing of a rich harvest, the seasonal showers, or an unexpected gift or inheritance; they all come from the hand of a God who does or permits them all. So what if we cannot prognosticate the outcome of all our joyful involvement in life's tasks? Is not this detail also covered in the plan of God? Men who insist on certainties or even just the most favorable conditions prior to acting in life never will do anything (11:4). The farmer who hesitates too much over threatening wind and clouds will never get down to sowing and reaping. Again, the duty is ours; the results are God's. Of course, this proverb must not be directed against careful observation of surrounding conditions. Rather, it is aimed at the fruitless and impossible demand for absolute certainty in conditions before we act.

In like manner 11:5 continues, saying that no one knows the way of the wind or the way bones are formed in a mother's womb; so it may be stated that even though the plan of God is known in general, "The work of God who accomplishes all" lies beyond our knowledge. No one can penetrate the wholeness or the specific details of His work. How God works out His purposes in detail may escape us, but our ignorance does not stop the result, nor should it prevent our wholehearted involvement in life to the glory of God.

Twice in verses 5 and 6 the phrase occurs, "You do not know." But the key to this section is the phrase in verse 6, "Withhold not your hand." Let the result—be it success or failure—rest in the hand of God. But do not just sit there, waiting for secure guarantees for life. Do something now, right where you are.

Thus Solomon has repeatedly coaxed, urged, argued, pressed, and begged us as wise men and women to get off the dead center of attempting to outguess God and His works. We must earnestly and diligently get into life's work. It is enough to know, as far as the progress and results of our work are concerned, that God is also at work. It is enough to know that He has given us the knowledge of the broad spectrum of His plan. Therefore, we will not deliberately withhold our energies or refrain from working. That small amount of admitted mystery in the divine plan will not hinder us from becoming active in life to the glory of God.

Questions for Discussion

1. Discuss the thrust of Ecclesiastes 9:10-12. What three arguments in 9:11-12 does Solomon present in support of his point?
2. List the five assets men enjoy. How valuable are those advantages and resources? Do they guarantee success?

3. Discuss the point of the parable in 9:13-16. What four conclusions may we draw from it?
4. Read Ecclesiastes 10:1-7. What key word emerges?
5. Discuss the five situations and corresponding dangers found in Ecclesiastes 10:8-10*b*. What makes the difference between success and failure in those situations?
6. From Ecclesiastes 10:12*b*-15*b* describe the characteristics of a fool, or one who does not exercise wisdom.
7. What is the common point of the six illustrations in 11:1-6? How are we to apply that point to the everyday business of living?

13

Death in View of God's Plan

ENJOY THE PRESENT AND LOOK FORWARD TO THE FUTURE (11:7-10)

Rejoice, shouts our learned guide, in all of life (11:7-9). Yet just as quickly he warns that the quality of life must be such that it will pass muster before the final Judge of all men and deeds. Our present life was meant to be joyous, as pleasant to the eyes as the rising sun in the morning light (11:7), but with the consciousness that we must render account unto God for all of life. And if we should live many years, verse 8 counsels that we should enjoy them all. Yet our eyes must be directed to those inevitable days of disease and death when we must go to the grave and then to meet our Maker and Fruit Inspector-Judge. Thus our writer begins his finale as he winds up his massive argument on God and culture, man and meaning.

Verse 9 has been taken in two different ways. Our view takes the phrase "Walk in the ways of your heart" as a direct contradiction of Numbers 15:39*b*: "You shall . . . not follow after your own heart and your own eyes" (cf. Deuteronomy 29:19; Job 31:7). Verse 9, however, is no contradiction to Numbers 15:39*b* or invitation to live sinfully in sensual pleasure.

The second view of 11:9 is to be preferred. It says the verse is an invitation to youth to get all the cheer and joy they can out of innocent happiness. Yes, enjoy whatever you see or desire, but *mark it down well* and in the midst of your enjoyment remember that God will review even the quality of your pleasures and the manner in which you enjoy yourself. Verse 9 is no carte blanche or open season in which *anything* goes. Therefore, do not abuse this blessing with evil comforts and pleasures that offer no real joy. Real but innocent and pure pleasures are recommended. Life must be lived with eternity's values in view. Your one life will soon be past, and only what is done for Christ and with eyes fixed on Christ will last. So have fun! Rejoice and delight yourself in the thrill of living. Yet put a prudent tone into your step by recalling that today will reappear in the tomorrow when we face the One who fully knows right from wrong.

Having shown in 11:7-9 that true happiness consists of simultaneously enjoying the present and looking forward to the future. Qoheleth now tells us how to regulate our lives accordingly. To enjoy true happiness we must remove all anxiety, sorrow, and sadness from our minds, for youth and life itself are so "transient," or "fleeting" *hebel,* 11:10). End all sadness, fretting, and morose gloom. Men must be free from those injuries to the inner man that so quickly cripple the joy of life.

REMEMBER TO LIVE FOR YOUR CREATOR BEFORE DEATH OVERTAKES YOU (12:1-7)

As Solomon concludes his treatise on how life is to be enjoyed as it was planned by God, he begs men

Death in View of God's Plan

and women to avoid future sorrow and evil by determining to "remember" their Creator in their youth (12:1). When he uses the word "remember," he is not asking for mere mental cognizance, for the biblical term "to remember" means much more than simple recall. Besides reflecting on and pondering the work of God in creating each individual and His world, there is the strong implication of action. For example, when God "remembered" Hannah (1 Samuel 1:19), He did more than say, "Oh, yes, Hannah; I almost forgot you." When He remembered her, He *acted* decisively on her behalf, and she who was barren conceived the child Samuel. So it is in our passage. To remember our Creator calls for decisive *action* based on recollection and reflection on all that God is and has done for us.

With one of the most beautiful of all allegories in the Scripture, using the picture of an old, decaying house, Qoheleth sets forth strong reasons for men and women to begin acting decisively in strenuous activity to the glory of their Creator *before* the evil days draw near. Indeed, already in 12:1 he has given three reasons why men must now work: (1) God is Creator of all; (2) He is their Creator; and (3) there are evil days coming when the body's strength and the mental capacities will begin to fail, and thus the output and potential for service to the living God will diminish significantly.

The next verses (12:2-6) detail this progressive dissipation in a most eloquent series of poetic pictures. Countless analogies have been suggested, but two principal ones usually emerge. One view sees verses 2-6 as a description of an approaching Palestinian storm that puts a stop to all business and causes all (masters, servants, men, women, and children alike) to quake. The second and more probably view, if a single interpretation of the analogy is to be used, is that the imagery of a decaying and unprotected house pictures the progressive decay that is coming on the bodily members.

The cloudy day following the showers in 12:2 is, according to the prevalent symbolism of the Old Testament, a day, or time, of pending misfortune (cf. Joel 2:2; Zephaniah 1:15). And the darkening of the sun, moon, and stars of verse 2, although more difficult to render than almost anything else in this allegory, possibly stands for those first signs of failure in a man's memory, understanding, will, affections, and imaginations. Delitzsche has a long proof in which he tries to equate "the sun" with the soul and "the moon" with the spirit, or principle of life in the body; and he says that "the stars" may refer to the five planets, that is, the five senses.[1] The attempt is ingenious enough, but it may be a bit overdone.

The general idea of what is happening in this verse can still be proclaimed, however: one *mental* and internal infirmity after another begins at the sunset of life (to use another metaphor), hampering our effectiveness in serving our Creator. Consequently, we would be well-advised to get moving ("remembering") while those evil days have not yet overtaken us.

In the next four verses (vv. 3-6) we have a list of *bodily* infirmities. These may be seen most easily in

---

1. Franz Delitzsch, *Commentary on the Song of Songs and Ecclesiastes*, trans. M. G. Easton (1877; reprinted in *Biblical Commentary on the Old Testament*, by C. F. Keil and Franz Delitzsch, Grand Rapids: Eerdmans, 1950), p. 404.

the following list of phrases, with the verse location in parentheses and the phrase's probable meaning in the right-hand column.

Allegory	Meaning
1. "Keepers of the house trembled." (3*a*)	1. The arms and hands tremble in old age with palsy or feebleness.
2. "Strong men are bent." (3*b*)	2. The legs are bent in feebleness, and the knees totter.
3. "Grinders cease, for they are few." (3*c*)	3. The teeth lose their ability to masticate food.
4. "Those looking out through the windows are dimmed." (3*d*)	4. The eyes begin to lose their sight, and the pupils become less dilated and more contracted.
5. "Doors are shut in the street." (4*a*)	5. The lips (swinging or folding doors, as the jaws of leviathan are called the "doors of his face" in Job 41:14) fall into the mouth for lack of teeth. (A street is a cleft between two rows of houses.)
6. "Sound of grinding is low." (4*b*)	6. In toothless old age, only soft foods may be eaten. Thus no noise is made, for no hard

Quality Living

Allegory	Meaning
	bread or parched corn is being chewed.
7. "One rises up at the voice of a bird." (4c)	7. The least amount of morning noise terminates his sleep.
8. "All the daughters of music are brought low." (4b)	8. The qualities (daughters) that make up the power to make and enjoy music and song are eluding him in his old age.
9. "They are afraid of what is high and terror shall be in the way." (5a-b)	9. He has developed a fear of heights and of stumbling along paths once familiar.
10. "Almond tree blossoms." (5c)	10. His hair has turned white with age.
11. "Grasshopper drags itself along." (5d)	11. Describes the halting gait of the elderly as they walk along on their canes.
12. "The caper berry fails to bear fruit." (5e)	12. All sexual power and desire is lost.
13. "Man goes to his eternal home while his mourners go about in the streets." (5f-g)	13. This phrase can be understood literally.
14. "The silver cord is snapped." (6a)	14. The spinal marrow connecting the brain and nerves is pale and silverlike.
15. "The golden bowl is broken." (6b)	15. This may be a reference to the brain

Allegory	Meaning
	because of its shape and color.
16. "The pitcher is broken at the fountain." (6c)	16. The failing heart, a pitcher-like receptacle, is pierced or broken, and all the life-supporting blood flows out.
17. "The wheel is broken at the cistern." (6d)	17. The system of veins and arteries that carries the blood around continually like a waterwheel breaks down when the heart breaks.

Then it is, after this slow dissolution has worked its evil, that the body made of earth returns to the earth (11:10). But the Spirit goes to God, who originally gave it to man. In a similar expression of confidence, our Lord yielded up His life, saying, "Into thy hands I commit my spirit" (Luke 23:46). So did Stephen: "Lord Jesus, receive my spirit" (Acts 7:59). Man has left this earth. True, his body is still in the soil, dissolving; but he is—actually—personally and consciously—present with God at that same moment.

All of this makes man's future perilous if he does not live in the knowledge that he will soon lose the privilege of working for his Creator.

Conclusions: Ecclesiastes 12:8-14

And so our writer concludes with the theme of his prologue (1:2): "Vanity of vanities, says Qoheleth; all is vanity." In other words, How futile to have lived and not to have known the key to living! What a waste to have died without having enjoyed life or known what it was all about. That is the tragedy of tragedies; a great waste. By repeating the second verse of the first chapter, Solomon indicates that he has concluded his treatise and is now ready to summarize everything.

The writer's qualifications for giving such instruction are next set forth in 12:9-10. In our judgment, this section also belongs to Solomon rather than to one of his "disciples" (as some would have it) who might have written on his behalf. The connection of verse 9 with verse 8 is clear from the conjunction "and," which begins verse 9 in the Hebrew text. The author laid claim to being "wise." Therefore his material was not the chatter of an experimenter or the musings of a "natural man." How could an unbeliever or a trifling experimenter be called wise?

Some may take exception to Solomon's calling himself "wise." But we would argue that the claim is couched in the third person instead of the first person, and the term "wise" marked him as a member of one of the three great institutions of his day: prophet, priest, and wise man (cf. Jeremiah 8:8-9; 18:18; Ezek. 7:26). The designation was a technical one, marking him as a member of the wise to whom God gave wisdom, just as the priest had the Law and the prophet had the Word. Therefore, his claim is no sign that he lacked modesty, for it is a claim that the wisdom in Ecclesiastes came from God in a revelation, just as the prophet's word also was given by divine inspiration.

Aside from the fact of his wisdom, "He continually

taught the people knowledge" with a deliberateness and care that merited his audience's most serious attention. There was a careful composing, investigating, and arranging of the proverbs and lessons he wrote. This was no haphazard spouting of negative thoughts in negative language. On the contrary, Solomon deliberately searched for "pleasant words," or "words of grace" (12:10). In no way can that be a description of the work of a pessimist, nihilist, or Epicurean with an "eat-drink-and-be-merry-for-tomorrow-we-die" mentality. Few passages in the Bible tell us more about the literary method used by the writer. His description removes all doubts about alleged hastiness of thought and expression. The result of his searching for the right words was that he communicated "words of truth" and not trite remarks. He wrote in "uprightness," that is, in perfect sincerity, without any pretense.

The function and source of Qoheleth's words are next set forth in verses 11-12. The imagery is taken from pastoral life: goads (wooden rods with iron points, used to prod the oxen into action or increased speed), nails (used by shepherd to fasten their tents), and the One True Shepherd are the means Solomon uses to make his points. Accordingly, Qoheleth's words are designed to prod the sluggish into action. They "goad" him into doing something. But they are also meant to be "nails" that are "fastened" as definite points in the sluggard's mental furnishings to give him anchorage, stability, and perspective on life. At one time they are pricking his conscience, perhaps with a single proverb; at another time they are fixing themselves on the memory like a central nail on which the important, everyday articles of clothing or cooking are kept. Some say Solomon's words are like a nail that is driven into a board to fix it in place. Those nails hold the "heads [lords] of collections" (v. 11), a reference, according to Genung, to those sayings that served as topic sentences, indicating the subject of each section or paragraph in which they stood.[2] Others (e.g., Leupold)[3] simply translate the expression as "collected sayings" to agree with the "words of the wise."

Another function found in Ecclesiastes is admonishment (v. 12). Whereas books may multiply and men may weary themselves with study of the ever enlarging library of volumes, the inspired words of Ecclesiastes will instruct, warn, and admonish. (The Hebrew word *zahar* does not appear in Proverbs, but it is found in Ecclesiastes 4:13, where it means "to take advice.")

Only one true source of the book could cause Solomon, the human author, to have such a high estimation of this book of Ecclesiastes: the "one Shepherd" (12:1). This can only mean Jehovah (or, more accurately, Yahweh), the Shepherd of Israel (Psalm 80:1). He is the real source of the words of this book; not cynicism, not skepticism, not worldliness—not any of these sources. He gave the ideas and aided Solomon in the composition of Ecclesiastes.

What then is the grand conclusion (end) of all these things? If we have been following our author's aim carefully, we should have added up all the parts of the

2. John F. Genung, *Words of Koheleth* (New York: Houghton, Mifflin, 1904), p. 359.
3. Herbert C. Leupold, *Exposition of Ecclesiastes* (Columbus, Ohio: Wartburg, 1952), pp. 296-97.

preceding argument and concluded that the chief end of man is to "fear God and keep His commandments, for this is the 'manishness' of a man and 'womanliness' of a woman" (12:13). What is the "profit" of living? What does a man get for all his work? He gets the living God! And his whole profit consists of fearing Him and obeying His Word.

What is more, "every work" and "every secret deed," no matter "whether it is good or whether it is bad" (12:14), will be brought under the searching light of God's judgment in that day when all men shall personally face Him to give an account of the deeds done in the body. So echoed Paul in 2 Corinthians 5:10. Men are responsible beings, not brutes, who are destined to live to confront the past with the God that they either feared or flouted.

No formula of legalism is this "keeping of His commandments." Neither is it a method of earning favor to be used when facing God. It is a summary of the beginning, middle, and end of life as we know it on this earth: coming to know and trust the living God; receiving the gifts of life's goods; learning how to enjoy those mundane gifts; understanding the major part of the plan of God; and being guided into joyous and strenuous activity in the art of living, even while portions of life remain enigmatic.

What a book! What a good God! What a life! And what a plan.

Questions for Discussion
1. According to Ecclesiastes 11:7-10, in what ways must we govern our enjoyment of life?

2. What is the significance of the word *remember* in 12:1?
3. Study the list of seventeen allegories in Ecclesiastes 12:1-6. Discuss the reasons Solomon gave for acting decisively for the glory of God.
4. What are the source and function of Qoheleth's words in 12:11-12?
5. Discuss how the conclusion of the four parts of the book add up to form the grand conclusion. What is the grand conclusion of the book of Ecclesiastes?

Selected Bibliography

Archer, Gleason. "The Linguistic Evidence for the Date of 'Ecclesiastes.'" *Journal of the Evangelical Theological Society* 12 (1969): 167-81. A good but technical study.

Breton, Santiago. "Qoheleth Studies." *Biblical Theology Bulletin* 3 (1973): 22-50. A survey of most recent commentaries and studies on Ecclesiastes, not including evangelical literature.

Delitzsch, Franz. *Commentary on the Song of Songs and Ecclesiastes.* Translated by M. G. Easton, 1877. Reprinted in *Biblical Commentary on the Old Testament,* by C. F. Keil and Franz Delitzsch. Grand Rapids: Eerdmans, 1950. A standard evangelical work for over a century.

Dreese, John J. "The Theology of Qoheleth." *The Bible Today*, November 1971, pp. 513-18. A good source of statistical studies on theological words.

Forman, Charles C. "Koheleth's Use of Genesis." *Journal of Semitic Studies* 5 (1960): 256-63. Very suggestive comparisons between the two books.

Ginsburg, Christian David. *The Song of Songs and Coheleth.* New York: Ktav, 1970. By far the most exhaustive discussion of the history of interpretation and grammatical points in Ecclesiastes.

Hengstenberg, Ernst Wilhelm. *Commentary on Ecclesiastes.* Translated by D. W. Simon. Philadelphia: Smith, English, 1860. An old but thoughtful Lutheran evangelical work.

Leupold, Herbert C. *Exposition of Ecclesiastes.* Columbus, Ohio: Wartburg, 1952. The best of all recent attempts to interpret the book. The writer, however, yields to spiritualizing tendencies in several spots and fails to offer a coherent argument for the whole book.

Shank, H. Carl. "Qoheleth's World and Life View as Seen in His Recurring Phrases." *Westminster Theological Journal* 37 (1974): 57-73. The repetitious vocabulary in Ecclesiastes is studied for possible patterns of interpretation.

Whybray, R. N. "Qoheleth the Immoralist? (Qoh. 7:16-17)." In *Israelite Wisdom: Theological and Literary Essays in Honor of Samuel Terrien,* edited by John G. Gammie. Missoula, Mont.: Scholars, 1978. Pp. 191-204.

Wright, J. Stafford. "The Interpretation of Ecclesiastes." *Evangelical Quarterly* 18 (1946): 18-34. The most impressive essay to appear on this book in this century. Also available in *Classical Evangelical Essays in Old Testament Interpretation,* Grand Rapids: Baker Book House, 1973, ed. W. C. Kaiser.

Wyngaarden, Martin J. "The Interpretation of Ecclesiastes." *The Calvin Forum* 19-21 (1953-55): 157-60. An interpretation that divides the book into "goads" and "nail" based on Ecclesiastes 12:11.

Moody Press, a ministry of the Moody Bible Institute, is designed for education, evangelization, and edification. If we may assist you in knowing more about Christ and the Christian life, please write us without obligation: Moody Press, c/o MLM, Chicago, Illinois 60610.